DCRM(S)

DESCRIPTIVE CATALOGING OF RARE MATERIALS (SERIALS)

·

Bibliographic
Standards Committee

Rare Books and
Manuscripts Section

Association of
College and Research
Libraries

IN COLLABORATION WITH

The Cataloging Policy
and Support Office
of the Library of
Congress

·

Cataloging Distribution Service
Library of Congress
Washington, D.C. 2008

For sale by the Library of Congress Cataloging Distribution Service, 101 Independence Avenue, S.E., Washington, D.C. 20541-4912. Product catalog available on the Web at <http:www.loc.gov/cds>.

ISBN: 978-0-8444-1217-7

This book is printed on acid-free paper.

Library of Congress Cataloging-in-Publication Data

Descriptive cataloging of rare materials (serials) / Bibliographic Standards Committee, Rare Books and Manuscripts Section, Association of College and Research Libraries in collaboration with the Cataloging Policy and Support Office of the Library of Congress.
    p.   cm.

"Descriptive cataloging of rare materials (serials) (referred to hereafter as DCRM(S)) is one of a family of manuals that form Descriptive cataloging of rare materials (DCRM), and is based on Descriptive cataloging of rare materials (books) (DCRM(B)), on the Anglo-American cataloguing rules, second edition, 2002 revision (AACR2), and subsequent updates, on ISBD(A) : International Standard Bibliographic Description for Older Monographic Publications (Antiquarian), second revised edition, 1991, on the CONSER cataloging manual (CCM), and on the CONSER editing guide (CEG) ... Previously, rules for cataloging rare serials were found in Appendix C of Descriptive cataloging of rare books, second edition (DCRB), published in 1991 by the Library of Congress"--Pref.

Includes bibliographical references and index.

ISBN: 978-0-8444-1217-7 (acid-free paper)

1. Cataloging of rare library materials--Handbooks, manuals, etc. 2. Cataloging of serial publications--Handbooks, manuals, etc. 3. Descriptive cataloging--Handbooks, manuals, etc. I. Association of College and Research Libraries. Rare Books and Manuscripts Section. Bibliographic Standards Committee. II. Library of Congress. Cataloging Policy and Support Office. III. Title: DCRM(S)

Z695.74 .D47 2008

025.3'416--dc22

2008025418

The front cover image is taken from *The flying-post, or, The post-master*, numb. 3257 (Tuesday, August 12 to Thursday, August 14, 1712), printed in London by William Hurt in 1712 (Beinecke Library shelfmark Z17 0176); the back cover image is of the tax-stamp on the same issue.

CONTENTS

PREFACE

Background

Descriptive Cataloging of Rare Materials (Serials) (referred to hereafter as DCRM(S)) is one of a family of manuals that form Descriptive Cataloging of Rare Materials (DCRM) (see introductory section I.1), and is based on *Descriptive Cataloging of Rare Materials (Books)* (DCRM(B)), on the *Anglo-American Cataloguing Rules,* second edition, 2002 revision (AACR2), and subsequent updates, on *ISBD(A): International Standard Bibliographic Description for Older Monographic Publications (Antiquarian)*, second revised edition, 1991, on the *CONSER Cataloging Manual* (CCM), and on the *CONSER Editing Guide* (CEG). DCRM(S) provides instructions for cataloging printed serials whose rarity, value, or interest make special description necessary or desirable.

Changes from DCRB

Previously, rules for cataloging rare serials were found in Appendix C of *Descriptive Cataloging of Rare Books*, second edition (DCRB), published in 1991 by the Library of Congress. That appendix was a revised version of the guidelines for treatment of rare serials published in the Library of Congress *Cataloging Service Bulletin* (CSB), no. 26, fall 1984. Cataloging a serial according to DCRB required the application of the appropriate areas of DCRB, namely 0-4 and 7. The most significant changes from DCRB are: new introductory sections on "Objectives and Principles" and "Precataloging Decisions;" the explicit incorporation of machine-made serials into the rule text and examples; expanded rules for determining the basis of the description; the addition of areas 3 and 6; an expanded appendix on early letter forms and symbols (including images of early letters and symbols accompanied by their correct transcriptions); and new appendixes on collection-level cataloging, variations requiring the creation of a new bibliographic record, reissued serials, and individual issues of serials.

DCRM(S) gives expanded guidance and prescribes a more rigorous and consistent approach to transcription than did DCRB, and incorporates a sharp distinction between information transcribed from the source and information that has been supplied by the cataloger. Transcribed information is never to be placed within square brackets (unless the letter or character is unclear; see 0G6.2). Conversely, the presence of square brackets in those areas of the description that require transcription (see introductory section III.2.2) immediately and unambiguously identifies text as supplied or interpolated. Another notable change related to more rigorous transcription principles is that roman dates in the source are transcribed as roman rather than arabic numerals.

Other changes include restricting transcription of the statement of responsibility to the chief source of information; the inclusion of dust jackets as a prescribed source of information for areas 2, 4, and 6; a discussion on the transcription of manufacturers in Area 4; the exclusion of copyright dates from the date of publication element; the elimination of special status for engraved title pages in the statement of extent; the dropping of periods after **cm** and **mm** (approved for AACR2 in 2002 but implementation deferred until publication in *RDA: Resource Description and Access*), and an expanded section on local notes. Area 0 is substantially re-organized, and the language throughout has been made more consistent and explicit.

Acknowledgments

DCRM(S) has been a long time coming. Jane Gillis, Rare Book Team, Yale University, and Juliet McLaren, ESTC, University of California, Riverside, spent many years developing the framework for the description of rare serials based on Appendix C of DCRB and taking the rules on the road in workshops and seminars. In 1998, when the Bibliographic Standards Committee decided to revise DCRB into DCRM(B), the rules for rare serials were put on the back burner. In January 2006, progress on DCRM(B) was far enough along that Committee attention could once again be turned toward serials and a DCRM(S) editorial board was appointed to complete the rules and mold them into a full-fledged DCRM component manual.

The DCRM(S) editors, who have given generously of their time, considerable knowledge, common sense, and editorial skills, are: Randal S. Brandt, Ann W. Copeland, Jane Gillis, Juliet McLaren, and Stephen Skuce. Four DCRM(B) editors have brought invaluable experience and expertise to discussions about rare serials: John Attig, Deborah J. Leslie, Joe A. Springer, and Manon Théroux.

Many others have contributed their time and effort in bringing DCRM(S) to fruition. Members of, and liaisons to, the Bibliographic Standards Committee since the DCRM(S) editorial board was formed in January 2006:

Marcia Barrett	Ryan Hildebrand	Stephen Skuce
Erin C. Blake	Deborah J. Leslie	James Stephenson
Randal S. Brandt	M. Winslow Lundy	Bruce Tabb
Ann W. Copeland	Juliet McLaren	Eduardo Tenenbaum
Laurence S. Creider	Kate Moriarty	Manon Théroux
David M. Faulds	R. Arvid Nelsen	Alex Thurman
Jain Fletcher	Margaret Nichols	Beth M. Whittaker
Jane Gillis	Elizabeth Robinson	
Eileen Heeran	Nina Schneider	

Sincere gratitude is extended to all those who, in addition to the above, contributed to DCRM(S) by participating actively at the public hearing, commenting on or proofreading drafts, and providing valuable research and expert opinion:

James Ascher	Edward T. Hoyenski	Carol E. Pardo
Morag Boyd	Elizabeth L. Johnson	Sara Piasecki
Alice Browne	Susan Karpuk	Nancy Mitchell
Ellen Cordes	Jim Kuhn	Poehlmann
Carroll Davis	Holley R. Lange	Freida Rosenberg
Christine DeZelar-	Faye R. Leibowitz	Joseph Ross
Tiedman	Martha Mahard	Jacquie Samples
Gerrit van Dyk	Maryvonne Mavroukakis	Elaine Shiner
Cynthia D. Earman	Robert L. Maxwell	Eileen L. Smith
Carol Fink	Morgan O.H. McCune	Amanda Sprochi
Nancy Frazier	Ann Myers	Susan Sundquist
Laura Hartman	Jennifer K. Nelson	Kay Teel

Conscientious and insightful comment on the final draft of DCRM(S) was provided by the ALA/ALCTS Committee on Cataloging: Description & Access (CC:DA), which charged a special task force to review the document: John Hostage, Jennifer Lang, Robert L. Maxwell, Helen F. Schmierer, and Elaine Shiner. Our partner in this publication, the Cataloging Policy and Support Office (CPSO) of the Library of Congress, also reviewed the text and made many influential suggestions courtesy of Judith A. Kuhagen and Barbara B. Tillett. Crucial, eleventh-hour advice relating to the alignment of DCRM(S) with CONSER was given by Valerie Bross, Les Hawkins, and Hien Nguyen.

A special debt of gratitude is owed to Judith A. Kuhagen, who took time to meet with the DCRM(S) editors in person several times and offered her expert opinion on more than a few particularly thorny issues.

Thanks also go to The Bancroft Library at the University of California, Berkeley, Beinecke Rare Book & Manuscript Library at Yale University, and the Folger Shakespeare Library for providing space and accommodations for DCRM(S) editorial meetings.

The index was prepared by Jean Skipp of IncludesIndex. The cover and title page design is by Kathy Bowlin of Graphic Answers Inc. All images come from the collections of the Folger Shakespeare Library and the Beinecke Rare Book & Manuscript Library at Yale University.

Randal S. Brandt
Chair, RBMS Bibliographic Standards Committee
12 August 2008

INTRODUCTION

Contents:

I. Scope and purpose

I.1. Descriptive Cataloging of Rare Materials

DCRM(S) is one of a family of manuals, each providing specialized cataloging rules for various formats of rare materials typically found in rare book, manuscript, and special collection repositories.[1] Together, these manuals form Descriptive Cataloging of Rare Materials (DCRM), an overarching concept rather than a publication in its own right.

I.2. Descriptive Cataloging of Rare Materials (Serials)

DCRM(S) provides guidelines and instructions for descriptive cataloging of rare serials, that is, printed textual serials receiving special treatment within a repository. DCRM(S) may be used for printed serials of any age or type of production. Electronic serials, with the exception of electronic reproductions of serials, are out of scope. For treatment of individual and special issues of serials, see Appendix H.

---

[1] The term "rare materials" is used to refer to any special materials that repositories have chosen to distinguish from general materials by the ways in which they house, preserve, or collect them. Rarity in the narrow sense of "scarce" may or may not be a feature of these materials.

I.3. Need for special rules

Printed materials in special collections often present situations not ordinarily encountered in the cataloging of typical modern publications (e.g., variation between copies, cancelled leaves) and may require additional details of description in order to identify significant characteristics (e.g., bibliographical format, typeface). Such details are important for two reasons. They permit the ready identification of copies of a resource (e.g., as editions, impressions, or issues), and they provide a more exact description of the resource as an artifact.

I.4. Scope of application

DCRM(S) is especially appropriate for the description of serials produced before the introduction of machine printing in the nineteenth century. However, it may be used to describe any printed serial, including newspapers, newsbooks, corantos, little magazines, and other periodicals.

These rules may be applied categorically to serials based on date or place of publication (e.g., all British and North American imprints published before 1831), or may be applied selectively, according to the administrative policy of the institution, which may choose to catalog some or all of its holdings at a more detailed level of description than that provided for in AACR2. (See introductory section X.1 for discussion on choosing appropriate cataloging codes and levels.)

I.5. Application within the bibliographic record

These rules contain instructions for the descriptive elements in bibliographic records only. They do not address the construction and assignment of controlled headings used as main and added entries, although brief instructions relating to headings and other access points do appear in some of the appendixes (e.g., Appendix F is entirely devoted to recommendations for uncontrolled title added entries).

II. Relationship to other standards

II.1. AACR2, ISBD(A), CONSER and other cataloging documentation

DCRM(S) is based on AACR2 as amended by the *Library of Congress Rule Interpretations* (LCRI), as well as on the second edition of ISBD(A) and on CONSER documentation. DCRM(S) deviates in substance from AACR2 and LCRI only when required by the particular descriptive needs of rare materials. In matters of style, presentation, wording, and subarrangement within areas, DCRM(S) follows its own conventions.

Refer to AACR2 and LCRI for guidance and instructions on matters of description not covered in DCRM(S). The relevant sections of AACR2 and LCRI must be consulted for rules governing name and uniform title headings to be used as access points for authors, editors, illustrators, printers, series, etc. For subject headings, numerous controlled vocabularies are available; within the United States, *Library of Congress Subject Headings* (LCSH) is widely used. Consult classification documentation for assignment of call numbers. For genre/form headings and relator terms, consult the various controlled vocabularies issued by the RBMS Bibliographic Standards Committee.[2] Terms from other authorized thesauri (e.g., Art & Architecture Thesaurus Online) may also be used as appropriate.

II.2. MARC 21

MARC 21 Format for Bibliographic Data is the presumed format for representation and communication of machine-readable cataloging. Use of DCRM(S), however, need not be restricted to a machine environment, and MARC 21 is not mandatory. Examples in the body of DCRM(S) are shown using ISBD punctuation; use of MARC 21 coding appears only in some of the appendixes. Catalogers using MARC 21 should follow MARC 21 documentation for input, and be aware of how their bibliographic systems interpret MARC 21 codes to automatically generate display features. This usually means, for example, that the cataloger omits punctuation between areas, parentheses enclosing a series statement, and certain words prefacing formal notes.

III. Objectives and principles

The instructions contained in DCRM are formulated according to the objectives and principles set forth below. These objectives and principles seek to articulate the purpose and nature of specialized cataloging rules for rare materials. They are informed by long-accepted concepts in bibliographic scholarship and the Anglo-American cataloging tradition, as well as by more recent theoretical work

---

[2] The RBMS Controlled Vocabularies include the following: Binding Terms; Genre Terms; Paper Terms; Printing and Publishing Evidence; Provenance Evidence; Relator Terms; and, Type Evidence.

important to the construction and revision of cataloging codes, namely the International Federation of Library Associations and Institutions' *Functional Requirements for Bibliographic Records* (FRBR) and Elaine Svenonius's *The Intellectual Foundation of Information Organization*. They assume familiarity with the FRBR terms used to categorize entities that are the products of intellectual or artistic endeavor (work, expression, manifestation, and item) as well as bibliographic terms used to differentiate among textual variants (edition, issue, impression, and state). It is hoped that these objectives and principles will provide catalogers, and administrators of cataloging operations, with a better understanding of the underlying rationale for DCRM instructions.

III.1. Functional objectives of DCRM

The primary objectives in cataloging rare materials are no different from those in cataloging other materials. These objectives focus on meeting user needs to find, identify, select, and obtain materials. However, users of rare materials often bring specialized requirements to these tasks that cannot be met by general cataloging rules, such as those contained in the latest revision of AACR2. In addition, the standard production practices assumed in general cataloging rules do not always apply to rare materials. The following DCRM objectives are designed to accommodate these important differences.

III.1.1. Users must be able to distinguish clearly among different manifestations of an expression of a work

The ability to distinguish among different manifestations of an expression of a work is critical to the user tasks of identifying and selecting bibliographic resources. In general cataloging codes like AACR2, it is assumed that abbreviated and normalized transcription is sufficient to distinguish among manifestations. Users of rare materials, however, often require fuller, more faithful transcriptions, greater detail in the physical description area, and careful recording of various distinguishing points in the note area, in order to identify separate manifestations. Additionally, users of rare materials are typically interested in drawing finer distinctions among variants within manifestations than are users of other materials, including not simply between editions and reissues but between variant impressions and states; many also need to distinguish between copies at the item level.

III.1.2. Users must be able to perform most identification and selection tasks without direct access to the materials

Users of rare materials frequently perform identification and selection tasks under circumstances that require the bibliographic description to stand as a detailed surrogate for the item (e.g., consultation from a distance, limited access due to the fragile condition of the item, inability to physically browse collections housed in restricted areas). Accuracy of bibliographic representation increases subsequent efficiency for both users and collection managers. The same accuracy contributes to the long-term preservation of the materials themselves, by reducing unnecessary circulation and examination of materials that do not precisely meet users' requirements.

III.1.3. Users must be able to investigate physical processes and post-production history and context exemplified in materials described

Users of rare materials routinely investigate a variety of artifactual and post-production aspects of materials. For example, they may want to locate materials that are related by printing methods, illustration processes, binding styles and structures, provenance, genre/form, etc. The ability of users to identify materials that fit these criteria depends upon full and accurate descriptions and the provision of appropriate access points.

III.1.4. Users must be able to gain access to materials whose production or presentation characteristics differ from modern conventions

In order to distinguish among manifestations, general cataloging codes like AACR2 rely on explicit bibliographic evidence presented in conventional form (e.g., a formal edition statement on the title page or its verso). In rare materials, such explicit evidence will often be lacking or insufficient to distinguish among different manifestations. That which is bibliographically significant may thus be obscured.

III.2. Principles of DCRM construction

To meet the objectives listed above, DCRM relies upon the following six principles. These principles are influenced by the general principles of bibliographic description offered by Svenonius: user convenience; representation; sufficiency and necessity; standardization; and integration.

III.2.1. Rules provide guidance for descriptions that allow users to distinguish clearly among different manifestations of an expression of a work

This principle derives from the general principle of user convenience and has implications for all areas of the bibliographic description. The principle relates to objective 1 stated above.

III.2.2. Rules provide for accurate representations of the entity as it describes itself, notably through instructions regarding transcription, transposition, and omission

This principle derives from the general principles of representation (with its related subprinciple of accuracy) and of standardization. Precise representation is of particular relevance in those areas of the description that require transcription (the title and statement of responsibility area, the edition area, the publication, distribution, etc., area, and the series area), but should not be ignored in the physical description and note areas. The general principles of representation and standardization stand in greater tension with each other when cataloging rare materials. Faithfulness to both principles may require descriptive and annotative treatment necessarily exceeding the norms (and at times the vocabulary) established as sufficient for the description of general materials. The principle relates to objectives 2 and 4 stated above.

III.2.3. Rules provide guidance for the inclusion of manifestation-specific and item-specific information that permits users to investigate physical processes and post-production history and context exemplified in the item described

This principle derives from the general principle of sufficiency and necessity (with its related subprinciple of significance). Application of the principle requires that rules for rare materials cataloging provide additional guidance on access points, particularly in cases where such information is not integral to the manifestation, expression, or work described. Rules for item-specific information appearing in the note area may recommend standard forms for presentation of information (addressing the general principle of user convenience and its related subprinciple of common usage). Application of such rules presumes both a user's need for such information and a cataloger's ability to properly describe such aspects. The principle relates to objective 3 stated above.

III.2.4. Rules provide for the inclusion of all elements of bibliographical significance

General cataloging codes like AACR2 routinely strive for both brevity and clarity, principles affiliated with the general principle of sufficiency. In describing rare materials, too great an emphasis on brevity may become the occasion for insufficiency and lack of clarity. Brevity of description may be measured best against the functional requirements of the particular bibliographic description rather than against the average physical length of other bibliographic descriptions in the catalog. The tension between rules for rare materials that promote accurate representation of an item and yet do not exceed the requirements of sufficiency is great. Reference to the principle of user convenience may offer correct resolution of such tensions. This principle is related to all of the objectives stated above.

III.2.5. Rules conform to the substance and structure of the latest revision of AACR2 to the extent possible; ISBD(A) serves as a secondary reference point

This principle relates to general principles of standardization and user convenience (with the latter's subprinciple of common usage). DCRM assumes that users of bibliographic descriptions constructed in accordance with its provisions operate in contexts where AACR2 (often as interpreted and applied by the Library of Congress) is the accepted standard for the cataloging of general materials. Therefore, DCRM uses existing AACR2 vocabulary in a manner consistent with AACR2; any additional specialized vocabulary necessary for description and access of rare materials occurs in a clear and consistent manner in DCRM rules, appendixes, and glossary entries. DCRM does not introduce rules that are not required by differences expected between rare and general materials. Numbering of areas within DCRM conforms to the structure of ISBD as implemented in AACR2. When an existing AACR2 rule satisfies the requirements of cataloging rare materials, DCRM text is modeled on AACR2 text (substituting examples drawn from rare materials for illustration). In cases where the language of AACR2 is not precise enough to convey necessary distinctions or may introduce confusion when dealing with rare materials, DCRM uses carefully considered alternative wording. Wording of relevant ISBD(A) standards was also considered when deviating from AACR2.

III.2.6. Rules are compatible with DCRB except in cases where changes are necessary to align more closely to current revisions of AACR2 or to conform to the above principles

This principle relates to general principles of standardization and user convenience (with the latter's subprinciple of common usage). DCRM assumes that users of bibliographic descriptions constructed in accordance with its provisions operate in contexts where serials in special collections were cataloged, until recently, using DCRB. Therefore, changes to DCRB cataloging practices were introduced into DCRM(S) only after careful consideration of the value or necessity of such changes.

IV. Options

Available options are indicated in one of three ways.

- ⸬ Alternative rule designates an alternative option which affects all or several areas of the description, and which must be used consistently throughout. In DCRM(S), alternative rules apply to the transcription of original punctuation and to the creation of separate records for individual impressions, states, binding variants, or copies.

- ⸬ *"Optionally"* introduces an alternative treatment of an element.

- ⸬ "If considered important" indicates that more information may be added in a note, and thus signals choices for more or less depth in the description. This phrase covers the entire range between best practice on the one end, and highly specialized practices on the other.

The cataloging agency may wish to establish policies and guidelines on the application of options, leave the use of options to the discretion of the cataloger, or use a combination of the two.

V. Language preferences

DCRM(S) is written for an English-speaking context. Cataloging agencies preparing descriptions in the context of a different language should replace instructions and guidelines prescribing or implying the use of English into their preferred language (see 4B3-4, 4B8-12, 4E, and areas 5 and 7).

VI. Spelling and style

DCRM(S) uses *Merriam-Webster's Collegiate Dictionary*, eleventh edition, as its authority in matters of spelling, and in matters of style, the fifteenth edition of the *Chicago Manual of Style*.

VII. Acronyms

AACR2	*Anglo-American Cataloguing Rules*, second edition
BDRB	*Bibliographic Description of Rare Books*
BIBCO	Monographic Bibliographic Program of the PCC
CC:DA	Committee on Cataloging: Description and Access, Association for Library Collections and Technical Services, American Library Association
CCM	*CONSER Cataloging Manual*
CEG	*CONSER Editing Guide*
CONSER	Cooperative Online Serials Program (Program for Cooperative Cataloging)
DCRB	*Descriptive Cataloging of Rare Books*
DCRM	Descriptive Cataloging of Rare Materials
DCRM(B)	*Descriptive Cataloging of Rare Materials (Books)*
DCRM(S)	*Descriptive Cataloging of Rare Materials (Serials)*
ISBD	*International Standard Bibliographic Description*
ISBD(A)	*International Standard Bibliographic Description for Older Monographic Publications (Antiquarian)*
LC	Library of Congress
LCRI	*Library of Congress Rule Interpretations*
LCSH	*Library of Congress Subject Headings*
PCC	Program for Cooperative Cataloging
RBMS	Rare Books and Manuscripts Section, Association of College and Research Libraries, American Library Association
RDA	*Resource Description and Access*

VIII. Examples and notes

VIII.1. Examples. The examples are not in themselves prescriptive, but are meant to provide a model of reliable application and interpretation of the rule in question. A word, phrase, element, or entire area may be illustrated; ISBD punctuation is given as needed only for the portion illustrated.

VIII.2. Notes. The instructions and guidelines in area 7 are written in imperative form. This does not imply that all notes are required; on the contrary, most notes are not (see 7A1.5). Consult the other areas of DCRM(S) in order to ascertain what is required and what is optional in any given situation (see 7A1). The conventions for notes included as part of the examples are as follows.

> ‣ *"Note"* indicates that the note is required if applicable to the situation.

> ‣ *"Optional note"* indicates that the note is not required. The labeling of a note as "optional" in these rules carries no judgment about its importance (see introductory section IV); certain notes designated as "optional" may in fact be almost universally applied.

> ‣ *"Local note"* indicates a note describing copy-specific information which is required if applicable to the situation (see 7B22).

> ‣ *"Optional local note"* indicates that the note concerns copy-specific information not affecting areas 1-6. It is not required, but must be clearly identified as a local note according to the provisions of 7B22.1.1. Copy-specific information that does affect areas 1-6, such as basing the description on an imperfect copy (see 0B2.5), is required and recorded in a general note.

> ‣ *"Comment"* prefaces details needed to adequately explain the example, and are not to be confused with notes appearing within the bibliographical description.

IX. Integrity of the copy

IX.1. Defects and sophistication

A greater vulnerability to damage, defect, and loss means that rare materials, especially older printed materials, are less likely than modern materials to be in a perfect or complete state when they reach the cataloger. One of the cataloger's tasks is to ascertain (within reasonable constraints) whether and how much the copy in hand deviates from its original state as issued. Imperfections and defects are usually easy to spot. Harder to spot during casual examination are replacement leaves, plates, or sections from another copy, and the cataloger is not expected to verify the integrity of each leaf in a publication unless there is reason to suspect that the copy in hand may have been made up, doctored, or falsified ("sophisticated"). Bibliographers' and booksellers' descriptions are the usual source of such information.

IX.2. Dust jackets

In the context of rare materials cataloging, dust jackets issued by the publisher are appropriately considered part of a serial, and are included in these rules as prescribed sources for areas 2, 4, and 6. Dust jackets often contain valuable information not found in any other source in the serial. Their easy detachability, however, coupled with their original function as protection for the binding only until it was safely in the hands of a reader, pose considerable difficulties for the rare materials cataloger. A fine dust jacket from a poor copy may have been exchanged with a poor dust jacket from a fine copy; the dust jacket of an original printing may end up on the copy of a later manifestation, and so on. When considering whether to transcribe information that appears only on a dust jacket, consider that the dust jacket was issued with the serial, unless there is reason to suspect otherwise.

X. Precataloging decisions

Before a bibliographic record can be created for a serial, or group of serials, awaiting cataloging in an institution's special collections, appropriate decisions must be made regarding the array of descriptive options available to the cataloger. These precataloging decisions include: determining whether DCRM(S) or AACR2 rules will govern the description, choosing the level of cataloging that will be applied, and determining the extent to which various options in the rules will be exercised.

Because DCRM(S) was written to address the special needs of users of rare materials, it is likely to be the appropriate cataloging code for the majority of printed serials held in special collections. However, for some categories of materials, the cataloging objectives (see introductory section III) may be met by use of AACR2 or by the application of options within the DCRM(S) rules that permit less detail in the description. Full-level DCRM(S) records that employ all possible descriptive options will not necessarily be the best choice for every serial.

The following section provides guidance for catalogers and cataloging administrators faced with these decisions and identifies some of the institutional and contextual factors that should be taken into consideration. It assumes that certain routine choices will already have been made, such as whether the encoding standard for the description will be MARC 21 and whether a resource issued as part of a monographic series will be analyzed.

Institutions may promote efficiency by setting cataloging policies for specific categories of materials in their collections rather than making decisions on an item-by-item basis. For example, an institution may decide to catalog all pre-1830 serials using DCRM(S), trace printers and booksellers for all pre-18th-century serials, but give signature statements and expansive descriptive notes for 17th-century serials only. It may choose to catalog all later serials according to AACR2, but add selected genre/form or provenance name headings. It may decide that collection-level cataloging is sufficient for brochures. A mechanism for easily making exceptions to general cataloging policy is desirable as well. If, for example, a curator buys a serial for its notable cloth binding, description of and access to the binding ought to be given in the bibliographic record, even if it is not the institution's usual policy to describe bindings.

X.1. Decisions to make before beginning the description

X.1.1. Item-level vs. collection-level description

Determine whether the material will receive item-level description, collection-level description, or some combination of the two.

Item-level cataloging represents the normative application of the DCRM(S) rules. Guidelines for creating collection-level descriptions are found in Appendix B. Collection-level cataloging is usually faster than item-level—sometimes dramatically so—but is attended by such a substantial loss of specificity that its use as the sole final cataloging for a group of items should be chosen only after careful consideration. The lack of specificity can be mitigated through provision of some sort of item-level control, such as an inventory list, finding aid, or database, and such an approach is highly recommended. Collection-level cataloging of rare materials is most suitable when items have minimal value in themselves but derive value as part of a collection. Use of collection-level control by itself may be appropriate when users are unlikely to be seeking known items, or the risk of inadvertent purchase of duplicate individual items is considered insignificant. Collection-level control alone is unlikely to provide adequate evidence to identify materials following a theft.

A combination approach would entail individual cataloging of all or selected items in the collection in addition to the creation of a collection-level record. Such an approach may involve phased processing, whereby the cataloger creates a collection-level record to provide immediate basic access to the collection, and then later creates item-level records for priority items as time and resources permit.

X.1.2. Cataloging code: AACR2 vs. DCRM(S)

Determine which cataloging code will govern the description. Both codes contain optional rules in addition to the required ones, and each allows varying levels of cataloging depth.

In item-level bibliographic records, use of AACR2 results in a description that highlights the common features of a serial and obscures some of the differences between manifestations or between variants of a single manifestation. AACR2 is generally considered to be easier and quicker to apply than DCRM(S). AACR2 is most suitable when, in an institutional context, a serial was acquired and is of significance primarily for its content rather than its artifactual value. In contrast, use of DCRM(S) produces more faithful transcriptions and more accurate physical descriptions. It will be more likely to facilitate differentiation between manifestations and reveal the presence of bibliographic variants among seemingly identical items. DCRM(S) is most suitable when a serial carries artifactual or bibliographical significance.

X.1.3. Serial vs. monograph

Determine whether the material will be cataloged as a serial, as a monograph(s), or as a combination of the two (see X.2.5).

A serial is a bibliographic resource issued in a succession of discrete parts, most frequently referred to as "issues." The issues usually bear numeric and/or chronological designations, and are intended to be published with no predetermined conclusion. Examples of serials include periodicals, journals, magazines, annual reports, newspapers, almanacs, monographic series, and society transactions.

Cataloging options:
- Catalog the issues collectively as a serial
- Catalog the issues individually as monographs (see Appendix H)
- Catalog the issues collectively as a serial and catalog some or all of the issues individually as monographs
- Create a collection-level bibliographic record for more than one serial with optional item-level records (see Appendix B)

X.1.4. Relationships to other serials

Serials may be related to one another in a variety of ways. Editions of a serial may be published concurrently, or nearly so, in different languages or different locations, or may be adjusted for a special audience.

Serials are also frequently reissued. A reissued serial normally appears after some time has elapsed since its original publication. It may have the same or a different title, have the same or a different publisher, distributor, etc., be issued in the same or a different place, or be reprinted in the same or a different format. The serial may be reissued so that the text is continuous, with one number following another on the same page, or the reissue may reproduce the style and appearance of the original serial (see Appendix J).

X.2. Factors to consider in making these decisions

Consider the following factors when determining appropriate levels of description and access for materials awaiting cataloging. These factors will help to identify items that might deserve more detailed descriptions or higher priority treatment, and assist in the decision to treat the resource as a serial or as a monograph.

X.2.1. Institution's mission and user needs

Evaluate the relevance of the items awaiting cataloging to the institution's mission and the needs of its users. Ideally, the institution will have developed internal documentation that will facilitate such an evaluation, including a mission statement, collection development guidelines, and a listing of constituent users and their anticipated needs. The needs of both patrons (researchers, teachers, students, etc.) and staff (collection development, reference, technical services, etc.) should be taken into consideration.

X.2.2. Institutional and departmental resources

Evaluate institutional and departmental resources, especially staffing levels, expertise, and current workloads.

- Is staff able to keep up with the inflow of new materials?

- Is there a reasonable balance between resources devoted to acquiring materials and those devoted to processing them?

- Is current staff expertise in languages, subject areas, descriptive standards, and encoding standards adequate for implementing and/or completing proposed work plans?

- › Is staff able to work concurrently with more than one code and/or description level?

- › Are funding and space available for hiring new temporary or permanent staff with the necessary qualifications?

- › Are adequate reference sources, such as specialized bibliographies, available for staff use?

- › How many other projects are in process and what are their requirements and priorities?

- › The regular review of cataloging priorities is highly recommended and should include discussions with curatorial, public services, technical services, and preservation staff.

X.2.3. Market value and conditions of acquisition of the item or collection

Consider the conditions of acquisition and the estimated market worth of the item or collection awaiting cataloging.

- › Does the monetary or public relations value of the material justify a higher level of access than would otherwise apply?

- › Have any access requirements been imposed by a donor as part of the terms of acquisition?

- › Is the item or collection accompanied by bibliographic descriptions that will facilitate cataloging?

X.2.4. Intellectual and physical characteristics of the item or collection

Finally, evaluate the intellectual and physical characteristics of the items awaiting cataloging.

- › Is there a unifying characteristic that would justify and facilitate the description of the materials as a collection (e.g., author, publisher, place of publication, genre/form)?

- › Is a particular collection renowned?

- › Do the materials have a topical focus that has recently acquired importance or urgency (e.g., due to a scholarly conference hosted by the institution or the hiring of a new professor with a particular specialty)?

› Is cataloging copy generally available?

› Were the items purchased primarily for their content?

› Do the specific copies have bibliographic or artifactual value?

› Is the institution collecting deeply in the area?

› Are detailed descriptions likely to reveal bibliographic variants that will be of interest to researchers?

› Are detailed descriptions likely to help prevent the inadvertent purchase of duplicates or the failure to acquire desirable variants?

› Is the item or collection vulnerable to theft or vandalism?

› Would a more detailed description help prevent unnecessary handling by staff and researchers?

X.2.5. Serial vs. monograph

Evaluate the advantages of cataloging an item as a serial or as individual monographs.

› Is cataloging copy generally available in either format?

› Do all the issues have either a date or enumeration?

› Can those items lacking a date or enumeration fit logically into a sequence?

› Does the title change with each issue?

› Would cataloging the item as a serial result in the loss of information or cause needless confusion?

› Would cataloging the item as a serial result in the loss of important subject access to individual issues?

› Would serials with analyzable titles, such as dime novels or auction catalogs, be better served by monographic records?

› Would cataloging individual issues as monographs cause needless repetition from record to record?

› Would cataloging individual issues as monographs place the serial title in an index of book titles where a researcher might not expect to find it?

0. General Rules

Contents:

0A. Scope

These rules provide instructions for cataloging printed serials whose rarity, value, or interest make special description necessary or desirable. They may be used in describing any printed serial, including newspapers, newsbooks, corantos, little magazines, and other periodicals. They cover instructions for the descriptive areas in bibliographic records only (see also introductory sections I-II). Individual and special issues of serials and unnumbered "special issues" may also be described as monographs (see Appendix H).

0B. The basic description

0B1. Required elements

The description must always include the following elements, to the extent possible, regardless of the completeness of the information available:

- ‣ title proper

- ‣ place of publication

- ‣ size

Also include other elements of description as set out in the following rules, if available and appropriate to the chosen level of description.

0B2. Basis of the description

0B2.1. General rule. Base the description of a serial on the earliest source associated with the whole serial or with a range of issues (e.g., a volume title page or the title page of a reissued serial). If no such source exists, base the description on the first or earliest available volume or issue.

0B2.1.1. Issues with volume title pages. For individual issues of one title bound with a volume title page, with or without prefatory material, indexes, appendixes, etc., base the description on the earliest volume title page. For cumulated issues of one title with contents physically rearranged, with or without additional text, base the description on the earliest volume title page.

0B2.1.2. Issues without volume title pages. For individual issues each having a title page, whether or not they are bound together, with no additional material, base the description on the earliest issue title page. For individual issues without individual title pages, whether or not they are bound together, base the description on the earliest issue.

0B2.2. Always make "Description based on" and "Latest issue consulted" notes (see 7B21).

0B2.3. For numbered serials, the first volume or issue is the lowest numbered volume or issue (or the volume or issue with the earliest chronological designation). For unnumbered serials, the first volume or issue is the volume or issue with the earliest publication, distribution, etc., date.

0B2.4. Serials may be issued bearing terms such as "premier," "introductory," or "pilot" issue. The issue may also carry regular numbering (e.g., "vol. 1, no. 1"). When an issue is truly the first issue (e.g., "premiere issue"), base the description on that issue. Do not, however, base the description on an issue that bears only wording such as "sample," "preview," or "trial," unless numbering on that issue, or on subsequent issues, confirms that it is truly the first issue. An issue that bears numbering that precedes "1," such as "vol. 1, no. 0," "no. 0," or "vol. 0," may be treated as the first issue when there is clear evidence that it is not merely serving as a sample issue. If a pilot or introductory issue precedes the true first issue of the serial, make a note, if considered important (see 7B9.4).

0B2.5. Imperfect copies. If the first volume or issue is lacking or imperfect, and no reliable description of it is available, base the description on the earliest available volume or issue that can supply the details necessary for the description. If a reliable facsimile (e.g., digital reproduction, microfilm) of the first volume or issue is available, use it as the basis of the description; use the earliest available volume or issue in hand to record other details of the description. If the only available volume or issue is imperfect, describe it as it is.

Make a general note to indicate that the description is based on an imperfect volume or issue.

0B2.6. Base the description of each specific area as follows:

Area	Basis of description
1. Title and statement of responsibility	First or earliest volume or issue
2. Edition	First or earliest volume or issue
3. Numbering	First and/or last volume(s) or issue(s) for each system or sequence
4. Publication, distribution, etc.	
Place and publisher, distributor, etc.	First or earliest volume or issue
Place and manufacturer	First or earliest volume or issue
Dates	First and/or last volume(s) or issue(s)
5. Physical description	All volumes or issues
6. Series	All volumes or issues
7. Note	All volumes or issues and any other source
8. Standard number and terms of availability	All volumes or issues and any other source

0C. Chief source of information

0C1. Single title page

The chief source of information is the title page, or, if there is no title page, the source from within the serial that is used as the substitute for it. If information traditionally given on the title page is given on two facing pages or on pages on successive leaves, with or without repetition, treat all of these pages as the chief source of information.

0C2. No title page

For serials issued without a title page (and for serials issued *with* a title page when the title page is missing and no reliable description of it is available), choose as the title page substitute one of the following, in this order of preference:

    a) analytical title page

    b) cover[3]

    c) caption

---

[3] Consider the cover to be a title page substitute only if it was issued by the publisher.

d) masthead

e) editorial pages

f) colophon

g) other pages

Always indicate in a note the source chosen as the chief source of information (see 7B3).

Hereafter in these rules, "title page" means "title page or title page substitute."

0D. Prescribed sources of information

The prescribed source(s) of information for each area of the description is set out in preferred order below. Do not transcribe any information not present in a prescribed source for that area.

Area	**Prescribed sources of information**
1. Title and statement of responsibility	Title page
2. Edition	Title page, other preliminaries, colophon, dust jacket (see introductory section IX.2)
3. Numbering	The whole serial
4. Publication, distribution, etc.	The whole serial
5. Physical description	The whole serial
6. Series	Series title page, serial title page, cover,[4] caption, masthead, editorial pages, colophon, dust jacket (see IX.2), rest of the serial
7. Note	Any source
8. Standard number and terms of availability	Any source

In all cases in which information for areas 1, 2, and 4 is taken from elsewhere than the title page, make a note to indicate the source of the information (see 7B6, 7B8, 7B10). In all cases in which information for area 6 is taken from elsewhere than the series title page, make a note to indicate the source of the information (see 7B14).

---

[4] Consider the cover to be a prescribed source only if it was issued by the publisher. Series-like statements present on covers not issued by the publisher usually represent binders' titles and should be treated as copy-specific information. They may be transcribed in a local note, if considered important. In case of doubt, do not consider the cover to be a prescribed source of information.

0E. Prescribed punctuation

Precede each area, other than the first, by a period-space-dash-space (. --) unless the area begins a new paragraph.

Precede or enclose each occurrence of an element of an area with standard punctuation as indicated in the "prescribed punctuation" sections of these rules.

Precede each mark of prescribed punctuation by a space and follow it by a space, with the following exceptions: the comma, period, closing parenthesis, and closing square bracket are not preceded by a space; the opening parenthesis and opening square bracket are not followed by a space.

End paragraphs with normal punctuation (usually the period).

If an entire area or element is omitted from the bibliographic description (e.g., because it is not present in the source), also omit its corresponding prescribed punctuation. Do not use the mark of omission.

0F. Language and script of the description

0F1. General rule

0F1.1. In the following areas, transcribe information from the serial itself in the language and script (wherever feasible) in which it appears there:

- › title and statement of responsibility[5]
- › edition
- › numbering
- › publication, distribution, etc.
- › series

0F1.2. Give interpolations into these areas in the language and script of the other information in the area, except for prescribed interpolations and other cases specified in these rules (e.g., 4B5, 4B6.2, 4C6.2). If the other information in the area is romanized, give interpolations according to the same romanization.

---

[5] If nonroman text has been transcribed within the first five words of the title proper, provide additional title access for a romanized form of the title proper (see Appendix F).

0F1.3. Give any other information (other than titles, citations, signatures, and quotations in notes) in the language and script of the cataloging agency.

0F2. Romanization

0F2.1. If it is not feasible to transcribe from the serial using a nonroman script, romanize the text according to the *ALA-LC Romanization Tables*. Do not enclose the romanized text within square brackets. Make a note to indicate that the romanized text appears in nonroman script in the serial (see 7B2.2).

> *Source:*
> ΕΡΜΗΣ ο῾ ΛΟΓΙΟΣ
>
> *Transcription:*
> ```
> Hermēs ho logios
> Note: Title in Greek script
> ```
>
> *Source:*
> Журнал геофизики и метеорологии
>
> *Transcription:*
> ```
> Zhurnal geofiziki i meteorologii
> Note: Title in Cyrillic script
> ```

0F2.2. *Optionally*, if it is feasible to transcribe from the serial using a nonroman script, also provide parallel romanized fields using the *ALA-LC Romanization Tables*. Do not enclose the romanized text within square brackets, but indicate in a note that the romanization does not appear in the source.

> ```
> Note: Romanization supplied by cataloger
> ```

0G. Transcription

Transcribe information in the form and order in which it is presented in the source, according to these general rules 0B-0G, unless instructed otherwise by specific rules. Do not use the mark of omission to indicate transposition.

0G1. Letters, diacritics, and symbols

0G1.1. Letters and diacritics. In general, transcribe letters as they appear. Do not add accents and other diacritical marks not present in the source. Convert earlier forms of letters and diacritical marks to their modern form (see Appendix G2). In most languages, including Latin, transcribe a ligature by giving its component letters separately. Do not, however, separate the component letters of æ in

Anglo-Saxon; œ in French; or æ and œ in ancient or modern Scandinavian languages. If there is any doubt as to the correct conversion of letters and diacritical marks to modern form, transcribe them from the source as exactly as possible.

0G1.2. Symbols, etc. Replace symbols or other matter that cannot be reproduced using available typographical facilities with a cataloger's description in square brackets. Make an explanatory note if necessary.

0G2. Capitalization and conversion of case

0G2.1. General rule. Convert letters to uppercase or lowercase according to the rules for capitalization in AACR2, Appendix A. Do not convert case when transcribing roman numerals.

0G2.2. Letters i/j and u/v. If the rules for capitalization require converting the letters **i/j** or **u/v** to uppercase or lowercase, follow the pattern of usage in the serial being described.[6] If the source uses a gothic typeface that does not distinguish between the letters **i/j** or the letters **u/v**, transcribe the letters as **i** and **v** respectively.

> *Source:*
> COMMERCIVM LITTERARIVM AD REI MEDICAE ET SCIENTIAE
>   NATVRALIS INCREMENTVM INSTITVTVM QVO QVICQVID
>   NOVISSIME OBSERVATVM AGITATVM SCRIPTVM VEL
>   PERACTVM EST SVCCINCTE DILVCIDE QVE EXPONITVR
>
> *Transcription:*
> ```
> Commercium litterarium ad rei medicae et scientiae naturalis
>     incrementum institutum quo quicquid nouissime obseruatum
>     agitatum scriptum vel peractum est succincte dilucide que
>     exponitur
> ```
> > (*Comment:* In the serial, the body of the text in roman type shows consistent use of v for vowels or consonants in initial position and u for vowels or consonants elsewhere, e.g., "vno," "vitae," "vniuersa," "quam," and "prouidentiae")

---

[6] For information on early printing as it pertains to the transcription of **i/j** and **u/v**, and guidance on how to determine the pattern of usage, see Appendix G4. If any of the letters is transcribed within the first five words of the title proper in converted form, provide additional title access using alternative forms of the title proper as needed (see Appendix F).

0G2.3. Chronograms. Capital letters occurring apparently at random or in a particular sequence on a title page or in a colophon may represent a chronogram. Where there is good reason to assume that a chronogram is being used, do not convert letters considered part of the chronogram from uppercase to lowercase, or from lowercase to uppercase (see also 4D2.2).

0G3. Punctuation in the source

0G3.1. General rule. Do not necessarily transcribe punctuation as it appears in the source. Instead, follow modern punctuation conventions, using common sense in deciding whether to include the punctuation, omit it, replace it, or add punctuation not present.

> *Source:*
>
> The genius of Albion: or, Weekly biographical, political, law, and literary repository

> *Transcription:*
> ```
> The genius of Albion, or, Weekly biographical, political, law and
>     literary repository
> ```

> *Source:*
>
> A AMSTERDAM, Chez WOLFGANG, WAESBERGE, BOOM, & van SOMEREN, M. D. C. LXXXVI.

> *Transcription:*
> ```
> A Amsterdam : Chez Wolfgang, Waesberge, Boom, & van Someren,
>     MDCLXXXVI [1686]
> ```

Alternative rule: Transcribe all punctuation as found in the source of information, with the exception of those marks covered in rules 0G3.5-0G3.7. When following this alternative rule, always include prescribed punctuation as well, even if this results in double punctuation. Prescribed punctuation is treated at the beginning of each chapter within these rules.

```
The genius of Albion: or, Weekly biographical, political, law,
    and literary repository
```
> (*Comment:* Commas are not required around *or* when applying this option; commas surrounding a conjunction introducing an alternative title are an AACR2 convention, not prescribed ISBD punctuation)

```
A Amsterdam, : Chez Wolfgang, Waesberge, Boom, & van Someren,,
    M.D.C.LXXXVI. [1686]
```

Descriptive Cataloging of Rare Materials (Serials)

0G3.2. Apostrophes. Transcribe apostrophes as found. Do not supply apostrophes not present in the source.

```
Cassel's family magazine

The will o' the wisp

Great Britaines paine-full messenger

Englands remembrancer of Lodons [sic] integritie, or, News from
    London
```

0G3.3. Hyphens. Transcribe hyphens used to connect the constituent parts of compound words, normalizing their form as necessary (see Appendix G2). Do not supply hyphens not present in the source.

```
The museum and Washington and George-town advertiser

Christmas news-boy

Report of the Boston Female Anti Slavery Society
```

0G3.4. Punctuation within roman numerals. Do not transcribe internal marks of punctuation appearing within roman numerals. Omit them without using the mark of omission.

Source:
M, DCC, LXXVIII

Transcription:
```
MDCCLXXVIII [1778]-
```

0G3.5. Ellipses, square brackets, and virgules. Do not transcribe ellipses ... or square brackets [ ] when present in the source; replace them with a dash -- and parentheses ( ) respectively or omit them, as appropriate. Do not confuse a virgule (/) in gothic typefaces with a slash; replace it with a comma or omit it, as appropriate. Make an explanatory note, if considered important.

Source:
Proceedings …

Transcription:
```
Proceedings--
```

0G3.6. Line endings. Do not transcribe a hyphen or other mark of punctuation used to connect a single word divided between two lines; transcribe as a single word, ignoring the punctuation. If the function of the hyphen is in doubt (e.g., if it might form part of a compound word), transcribe it.

> *Source:*
> Severall
> New and good Passa-
> ges, or the weekly procee-
> dings from the divers places in this King-
> dome
>
> *Transcription:*
> ```
> Severall new and good passages, or, The weekly proceedings from
>     the divers places in this kingdome
> ```

0G3.7. Punctuation substituting for letters. Transcribe as hyphens any hyphens, dashes, or underscore characters used in the source as a substitute for one or more letters in a word or an entire word. Use one hyphen for each distinct piece of type.

> *Source:*
> Sec--t----s of st-te, the L--ds of the Ad-----ty
>
> *Transcription:*
> ```
> Sec--t----s of st-te, the L--ds of the Ad-----ty
> ```

Transcribe asterisks as asterisks.

> ```
> par Mr. B***
> ```

If the values of the missing letters are known, provide the information in a note.[7]

> *Source:*
> The r --- l register: with annotations by another hand
>
> *Transcription:*
> ```
> The r---l register : with annotations by another hand
> ```
> *Note:* The r---l register is The royal register

---

[7] If punctuation substituting for letters occurs in the first five words of the title proper, and the values of the missing letters are known, provide additional title access for the decoded form of the title proper (see Appendix F).

0G4. Spacing

0G4.1. Spacing within words and numbers. In general, follow modern spacing conventions when transcribing from the source. Make no attempt to preserve full or irregular spaces between letters within words. If a word is divided between the end of one line and the beginning of the next, transcribe it as a single word, ignoring the line-break.

Omit internal spaces when transcribing numbers (including roman numerals).

> *Source:*
> C I T Y JACKDAW

> *Transcription:*
> ```
> City jackdaw
> ```

> *Source (showing line endings):*
> CATALOGVS VNI-
> VERSALIS PRO NVN -
> DINIS FRANCOFVRTENSI-
> bus vernalibus de anno …

> *Transcription:*
> ```
> Catalogus vniuersalis pro nundinis Francofurtensibus vernalibus
>    de anno ...
> ```

Alternative rule: Transcribe internal spaces within numbers (including roman numerals). If multiple spaces or different sizes of spaces appear between two characters within the number, transcribe them as a single space.

> *Source:*
> M. D. CC. XLIV.

> *Transcription:*
> ```
> M. D. CC. XLIV.
> ```

0G4.2. Spacing between words. If spacing between words in the source is ambiguous, or lacking, include spaces in the transcription to separate the words as needed.[8]

> *Source:*
> The DUTCHSPY
>
> *Transcription:*
> ```
> The Dutch spy
> ```
>
> *Source:*
> CALIFORNIAPRINTMAKER
>
> *Transcription:*
> ```
> California printmaker
> ```

0G4.3. Variant spellings. Do not insert spaces within single words that merely represent variant or archaic spellings.[9]

> *Source:*
> Newhampshire & Vermont ALMANAC
>
> *Transcription:*
> ```
> Newhampshire & Vermont almanac
> ```

0G5. Omissions

0G5.1. General rule. Indicate omissions in the transcription or in a quoted note by using the mark of omission. When using the mark of omission, generally give it with a space on either side. However, give a space on only one side if the mark comes at the end of an area, is preceded by an opening parenthesis or opening square bracket, or is followed by a closing parenthesis, closing square bracket, or comma.

> ```
> London : Printed and sold by Charles Lillie ... and John Morphew,
>    1710-1712
> ```

---

[8] If the missing spaces occur in the first five words of the title proper, provide additional title access for the form of title as it appears in the source, without the spaces (see Appendix F).

[9] If the variant or archaic spellings occur in the first five words of the title proper, provide additional title access for the form of the title with the spacing inserted (see Appendix F).

```
Dublin : Printed by P. Byrne ..., 1788
```
>(*Comment:* The mark of omission has a space on only one side because it is followed by a comma)

0G5.2. Information not considered part of any area. If omitting grammatically separable information from the transcription because it is not considered part of any area (pious invocations, etc.; see 1A2.2), do not use the mark of omission. If considered important, give the omitted information in a note.

0G5.3. Information not taken from the chief source of information. If transcribing information from a source other than the chief source of information, omit any words preceding or following the information if they are not considered part of the element and are grammatically separable. Do not use the mark of omission. If considered important, give the omitted text in a note.

```
Centenary edition
Note: Edition statement from t.p. verso; full statement reads:
   "This centenary edition is strictly limited to 350 copies"
```

0G6. Interpolations

0G6.1. General rule. Indicate an interpolation in the transcription or in a quoted note by enclosing it in square brackets. If transcribing text with missing or obscured letters or words that can be reconstructed with some certainty, include these in the transcription, enclosing them in square brackets. Make an explanatory note, if considered important.

```
The Antigua merc[ury, or,] St. John's weekly adve[rtiser]

Whal[ley's] news-le[tt]er
```
>(*Comment:* Issue mutilated at head, affecting title)

0G6.2. Conjectural and indecipherable text. Indicate a conjectural interpolation by adding a question mark immediately after the interpolation, within square brackets. Supply a question mark enclosed in square brackets for each indeterminable word or portion of word. Make notes to justify the interpolations, provide explanations, or offer tentative readings of indecipherable portions of text, if considered important.

0G6.3. Lacunae in imperfect copies. If the description is based on an imperfect copy (see 0B2.5), use the mark of omission enclosed in square brackets ([...]) to show lacunae in the resource.

```
Norimberga[e] : Sumptibus Societa[tis], litteris Joh. Ernesti
   Ad[...]
Note: Description based on an imperfect copy; title page torn
   with partial loss of imprint
```

0G6.4. Adjacent elements within a single area. If adjacent elements within one area are to be enclosed in square brackets, generally enclose them in one set of square brackets.

```
[Portsmouth : G.H. Mottley and W. Harrison]
```

If the square brackets are due to interpolations such as corrections or expansions (see 0G8, 4B3, 4B4, 4B5), however, use separate pairs of square brackets.

```
Salem [Mass.] : [Mary Crouch & Co.]
```

0G6.5. Adjacent elements in separate areas. If adjacent elements are in different areas, enclose each element in a set of square brackets.

0G7. Misprints, etc.

0G7.1. Misprints. Transcribe a misprint as it appears in the serial. Follow such an inaccuracy either by "[sic]" or by the abbreviation "i.e." and the correction within square brackets.[10]

```
Police regulations for the Amry [sic] of the District of Eastern
   Arkansas

Constitutionalsit [sic]—Extra

Archivum eurasiae medii aeivi [i.e. aevi]
```

Do not correct words spelled according to older or non-standard orthographic conventions (e.g., "françoise" for "française," "antient" for "ancient," "Aufflage" for "Auflage").

0G7.2. Turned and approximated letters. Transcribe a turned letter (i.e., a letter set upside-down), whether inadvertent or deliberate, as the intended letter. Transcribe two letters used to approximate a third letter as the intended letter.

---

[10] If the misprint occurs in the first five words of the title proper, provide additional title access for the form of title without the interpolation and for the form of title as if it had been printed correctly (see Appendix F).

However, transcribe **vv** as **vv** (see Appendix G5). Make an explanatory note, if considered important.[11]

```
London
Optional note: First "n" in "London" printed with a turned "u"

Wittenberg
Optional note: The "W" in "Wittenberg" is formed using "rv"

The kingdomes vveekly intelligencer
```

0G8. Abbreviations and contractions

0G8.1. When transcribing from the serial, do not abbreviate any words not abbreviated in the source.

0G8.2. If special marks of contraction have been used by the printer in continuance of the manuscript tradition, expand affected words to their full form and enclose supplied letters in square brackets (see Appendix G3). Make an explanatory note, if considered important (see 7B4.1.2). If a contraction standing for an entire word appears in the source, supply instead the word itself, enclosed in square brackets. However, transcribe an ampersand or a Tironian sign (**7**) as an ampersand. Enclose each expansion or supplied word in its own set of square brackets.

If the meaning of a contraction is conjectural, apply the bracketing conventions given in 0G6.2.

0G9. Superscripts and subscripts

Transcribe superscript and subscript characters on the line unless the sense would be affected (e.g., in a mathematical formula).

Source:
McDonnell's weekly Dublin journal

Transcription:
```
McDonnell's weekly Dublin journal
```

---

[11] If the two letters used to approximate a third letter occur in the first five words of the title proper, provide additional title access for the form of title with the letters transcribed as set (see Appendix F).

0G10. Initials, etc.

0G10.1. Transcribe initials, initialisms, and acronyms without internal spaces, regardless of how they are presented in the source of information.

```
R.L. Polk & Co.'s directory of Olympia, Port Townsend, Fairhaven,
   New Whatcom and Whatcom

A.B.C. indicateur alphabetique des chemins de fer et de la
   navigation
```

0G10.2. Treat an abbreviation consisting of more than a single letter as if it were a distinct word, separating it with a space from preceding and succeeding words or initials.

```
Mr. J.P. Morgan
```

0G10.3. If two or more distinct initialisms (or sets of initials), acronyms, or abbreviations appear in juxtaposition, separate them with a space.

```
M. J.P. Rabaut
```
       (*Comment:* The first initial stands for Monsieur)

1. Title and Statement of Responsibility Area

Contents:

1A. Preliminary rule

1A1. Prescribed punctuation

For instructions on the use of spaces before and after prescribed punctuation, see 0E.

Precede the title of a supplement or section (see 1B5), or the designation for a supplement or section, by a period.

Precede the title of a supplement or section following a designation for the supplement or section by a comma.

Precede each parallel title by an equals sign.

Precede each unit of other title information by a colon.

Precede the first statement of responsibility by a diagonal slash.

Precede each subsequent statement of responsibility by a semicolon.

1A2. Sources of information

1A2.1. General rule. The prescribed source of information for the title and statement of responsibility area is the title page.

1A2.2. Omission of pious invocations, etc. Omit, without using the mark of omission, information found on the title page that constitutes neither title information nor a statement of responsibility. Such information may include pious invocations, quotations, devices, announcements, epigrams, mottoes, prices, etc. (see 0G5.2). Transcribe or describe this kind of information in a note, if considered important. If such information is a grammatically inseparable part (see 1B1) of one of the elements of the title and statement of responsibility area, however, transcribe it as such. If such information constitutes the only title-like information present in the source, it may be used as a devised title according to the provisions of 1B4.

1A3. Form and order of information

Transcribe title and statement of responsibility information in the form and order in which it is presented in the source, unless instructed otherwise by specific rules (see 0G).

1B. Title proper

1B1. Words considered part of the title proper

1B1.1. The title proper is the first element of the description. Title information preceding the chief title on the title page is considered part of the title proper. If the chief title is preceded or followed in the source by other elements of information, transpose these elements to their appropriate areas in the description (or give them in a note) unless case endings would be affected, the grammatical construction of the information would be disturbed, or the text is otherwise grammatically inseparable from the title proper. In the latter cases, transcribe the information as part of the title proper.

```
Journal des dames et des modes

Brown's industrial gazetteer and hand-book of the Atchison,
    Topeka & Santa Fe R.R.

The South-Carolina state gazette, and general advertiser

Transactions of the society, instituted at London, for the
    encouragement of arts, manufactures, and commerce

Annual report of the Gloucester Fishermen's Institute,
    Gloucester, Mass.

Number ... of A picture of the times, to be continued weekly, in
    a series of letters, addressed to the people of England
```

1B1.2. Make a note to indicate the original position on the title page of transposed elements (see 7B4.1.2).

Source:
Head Quarters, Dist. of Texas, New Mexico and Arizona, Houston, Texas … Special orders no. …

```
Special orders no. ... / Head Quarters, Dist. of Texas, New
    Mexico and Arizona, Houston, Texas ...
Note: Statement of responsibility transposed from head of title
```

1B1.3. When the title appears in full and in the form of an acronym or initialism in the chief source of information, choose the full form as the title proper (see also 1D2).[12]

Source:
BLM Bonniers litterära magasin

Transcription:
```
Bonniers litterära magasin : BLM
Note: Title page reads: BLM Bonniers litterära magasin
```

1B1.4. In case of doubt about whether a name or an abbreviation of that name, or any word, phrase, or other statement, is part of the title proper, treat the name or phrase as part of the title proper only if it is consistently so presented in various locations in the serial and/or as found in indexes, abstracts, or other sources.

Source:
W.B. Cummings & Co. market review

Transcription:
```
W.B. Cummings & Co. market review
```

Source:
R.L. Polk & Co.'s Des Moines city and Polk County directory

Transcription:
```
R.L. Polk & Co.'s Des Moines city and Polk County directory
```

1B2. Note on the source of the title proper

Always make a note on the source of the title proper (see 7B3). Combine the "Source of title" note with the "Description based on" note (see 7B21.1).

```
Pacific stomatological gazette : a monthly magazine devoted to
    dental science and literature
Note: Description based on: Volume IV; title from title page
```

---

[12] When choosing the full form as the title proper, provide additional title access for the acronym or initialism (see Appendix F).

```
Gazette littéraire de l'Europe
Note: Description based on: Tome premier (comprenant les mois de
   mars, avril & mai 1764); title from title page

Whiston's merchants weekly remembrancer of the currant present-
   money-prices of their goods ashoar in London ...
Note: Description based on: Monday, June 17th, 1689; title from
   caption

Mercurius aulicus : communicating the intelligence and affaires
   of the court to the rest of the kingdome
Note: Description based on: The first weeke ([1-8 Jan. 1643]);
   title from caption
```

1B3. Forms of the title proper

The title proper can take a variety of forms, some of which are exemplified below:

1B3.1. Title proper inclusive of alternative titles:

```
The night-walker, or, Evening rambles in search after lewd women

La quotidienne, ou, La feuille du jour

Parnassus boicus, oder, Neu-eröffneter Musen-Berg

The Boston gazette, or, New-England weekly journal
```

1B3.2. Title proper consisting solely of the name of a responsible person or body:

```
American Tract Society

The Aldine

New England Loyal Publication Society
```

1B4. No title proper

If no title can be found in any source, devise a brief descriptive title, preferably in the language and script of the cataloging agency, and use this devised title, enclosed in square brackets, as the title proper. Indicate in a note that the title has been devised by the cataloger.

```
[East India Company regulations, Bombay, India]
Note: Description based on: VI; title devised from content
      (Comment: Only numbering appears on t.p.)
```

1B5. Title proper with supplementary or section designation or title

If the title proper for a work that is supplementary to, or a section of, another work appears in two or more grammatically separable parts, transcribe the title of the main work first, followed by the designation(s) and/or title(s) of the supplement(s) or section(s) in order of their dependence. Make a note to indicate the original position on the title page of any transposed elements.

```
Boletim. Nova série, Antropologia

Études et documents tchadiens. Série B
Note: "Série B" transposed from head of title
```

1B6. Abridgments of the title proper

1B6.1. General rule. Abridge a long title proper only if it can be done without loss of essential information. Do not omit any of the first five words. Indicate omissions by the mark of omission.

```
Annual report of the Board of Directors of the St. Louis, Alton,
    and Terre Haute Rail-road Company ...
```

1B6.2. Alternative title. If the title proper contains an alternative title, do not omit any of the first five words of the alternative title.

```
The political history of Europe, or, A faithful and exact
    relation of the present state of the church and religion ... :
    with an account of new books

The phenix, or, A revival of scarce and valuable pieces ...

Bibliothèque britannique, ou, Recueil extrait des ouvrages
    anglais périodiques ... : des mémoires et transactions des
    sociétés et académies de la Grande-Bretagne, d'Asie, d'Afrique
    d'Amérique
```

1B6.3. Chief title. Extend the transcription of the title proper at least through the end of the chief title of the resource. Apply this provision even if other words in the title proper precede the chief title (see 1B1.1).

```
Price guide presents-- Muscle car and truck buyer's guide
```
            (*Comment:* The chief title is "Muscle car and truck buyer's guide")

If the end of the chief title cannot be determined, break off the transcription at the first grammatically acceptable place, but in no event within the first five words of the chief title.

1B6.4. Omission of dates, names, numbers, etc. If the title proper includes a date, name, number, etc., that varies from issue to issue, omit this date, name, number, etc., and replace it by the mark of omission. Make a note describing omitted information, if considered important.

Source:

Report of the 29th annual Lake Mohonk Conference of Friends of the Indian and Other Dependent Peoples

Transcription:
```
Report of the ... annual Lake Mohonk Conference of Friends of the
   Indian and Other Dependent Peoples
```
Optional note: The word "annual" in the title is preceded by "1st," "2nd," etc.

Source:

Annual report of Hon. Edward M. Stanton, Secretary of War, for the year 1866

Transcription:
```
Annual report of ... Secretary of War, for the year ...
```
Optional note: Name of the Secretary of War appears in each title

Source:

Fifth annual address of the carriers of the Salem gazette and Essex county mercury to their patrons

Transcription:
```
... Annual address of the carriers of the Salem gazette and Essex
   county mercury to their patrons
```
Optional note: Title begins with ordinal designation

1B7. Change in title proper

If a major change in the title proper occurs, make a new description (see Appendix E). If a minor change occurs in the title proper on a subsequent volume or issue, in general, give the later title in a note (see 7B4.3).

1C. Parallel titles

1C1. Order and source of parallel titles

Transcribe parallel titles in the order indicated by their sequence on, or by the layout of, the title page. If the original title appears elsewhere than on the title page, transcribe it in a note, if considered important.

1C2. Language of parallel titles and relationship to title proper

1C2.1. Transcribe an original title in a language different from that of the title proper appearing on the title page as a parallel title, unless it is grammatically inseparable from another part of the description.

```
Il mercurio italico, o sia, Ragguaglio generale intorno alla
    letterature, belle arti, utili scoperte, ec. di tutta l'Italia
    = The Italian mercury, or, A general account concerning the
    literature, fine arts, useful discoveries, &c. of all Italy
```

1C2.2. Transcribe as other title information an original title in the same language as the title proper (see 1D).

1C2.3. If a parallel title is added, deleted, or changed on a subsequent volume or issue, make a note if the change is considered important (see 7B5.2).

1D. Other title information

1D1. Order and source of other title information

Transcribe other title information appearing on the title page in the order indicated by the sequence on, or layout of, the title page. Transcribe other title information not appearing on the title page in a note, if considered important.

```
Sur le dos de la tortue : revue bilingue de littérature
    amérindienne
```

1D2. Transposition of other title information

If other title information precedes the title proper in the source, transpose it to its required position. When transposing other title information, do not use the mark of omission. Make a note indicating the transposition (see 7B4.1.2).

```
Bonniers litterära magasin : BLM
Note: Title page reads: BLM Bonniers litterära magasin

The Agorá : a Kansas magazine
Note: On t.p., "A Kansas magazine" appears at head of title
```

1D3. Other title information beginning with prepositions, conjunctions, etc.

1D3.1. General rule. Transcribe title information that appears following the title proper as other title information, even if it begins with a preposition, conjunction, prepositional phrase, etc.

```
Tucson and Tombstone general and business directory for ... :
   containing a complete list of all the inhabitants, with their
   occupations and places of residence, the public officers,
   secret societies and churches, together with other useful
   information concerning both cities
```

1D3.2. If this other title information appears following the statement of responsibility, transcribe it as a subsequent statement of responsibility (see 1E14.2).

1D3.3. If this other title information, or some portion of it, constitutes a formal statement of the contents of the work that remains the same from issue to issue and is grammatically separable from the title proper and other title information, transcribe it in a note, if considered important (see 7B19.2). When these formal statements are omitted from the title and statement of responsibility area, use the mark of omission.

```
The treble almanack for the year ... : containing ...
Optional note: Contents: (from t.p.) I. John Watson Stewart's
   almanack -- II. Exshaw's English court registry -- III.
   Wilson's Dublin directory with a new correct plan of the city,
   forming the most complete lists published of the present civil,
   military and naval establishments of Great Britain & Ireland
```

1D4. Statements about illustrations or volumes

Treat an illustration statement or a statement such as "in two volumes" as other title information, unless the statement is grammatically inseparable from information transcribed as part of another element or area (see 1E13 and 2B5). If the statement appears following the statement of responsibility, transcribe it as a subsequent statement of responsibility.

```
A journal of natural philosophy, chemistry, and the arts :
   illustrated with engravings / by William Nicholson

The theatrical inquisitor, or, Literary mirror / by Cerberus ...
   ; embellished with superb engravings

The true Briton : in two volumes ...

The idler / by the author of The rambler ; with additional essays
   ; in two volumes
```

1D5. Abridgment of other title information

Optionally, if other title information is very lengthy and can be abridged without loss of essential information, omit less important words or phrases, using the mark of omission. If considered important, transcribe omitted words or phrases in a note (including the other titles or phrases referred to in 1D3.3).

```
The universal magazine of knowledge and pleasure : containing
    news, letters, debates, poetry, music ... and other arts and
    sciences ... : to which occasionally will be added an impartial
    account of books in several languages ...
```

1D6. Statements about earlier titles, etc.

Treat a statement containing an earlier title, an absorbed title, etc., as other title information unless it is grammatically inseparable from the title proper or another part of the description. Give relationships with other serials in a note (see 7B7).

Source:

Jackson's Oxford gazette and news, formerly Flynn's Oxford gazette

Transcription:
```
Jackson's Oxford gazette and news : formerly Flynn's Oxford
    gazette
```

Source:

The Trow (formerly Wilson's) copartnership and corporation directory of New York City

Transcription:
```
The Trow (formerly Wilson's) copartnership and corporation
    directory of New York City
```

1D7. Other title information with grammatically inseparable elements

If the other title information includes a statement of responsibility or an element belonging to another area, and the element is a grammatically inseparable part of the other title information according to one or more of the conditions enumerated in 1B1.1, transcribe it as other title information.

```
American pioneer : a monthly periodical, devoted to the objects
    of the Logan Historical Society, or to collecting and
    publishing sketches relative to the early settlement and
    successive improvement of the country
```

1D8. Parallel statements containing other title information

Transcribe parallel statements containing other title information in the order in which they appear on the title page.

1D9. Change in other title information

If other title information has been recorded in the title and statement of responsibility area and that information changes in a subsequent issue, make a note if the change is considered important.

1E. Statements of responsibility

1E1. Statements of responsibility on the title page

1E1.1. Transcribe statements of responsibility appearing on the title page in the form in which they appear.

```
The American law journal and miscellaneous repertory / by John E.
   Hall

The American medical and philosophical register, or, Annals of
   medicine, natural history, agriculture and the arts / conducted
   by a society of gentlemen

The connoisseur / by Mr. Town, critic and censor-general

The German correspondent / by Hermann

 Mercurius Britannicus : being collections of publick
   intelligence ... / by Walter Campbell

The spring-garden journal / by Miss Priscilla Termagant (a near
   relation of the late Mrs. Roxana)
```

1E1.2. *Optionally*, do not transcribe statements relating to persons named as editors[13] as statements of responsibility. If a statement relating to an editor is considered important, give it in a note (see 7B6.1). Indicate the omission by the mark of omission.

```
Note: Editors: 1680-1738, Jean-Alexandre de La Font; 1738-1798,
   Etienne Luzac (with Jean Luzac, 1772-1798); 1798-1811, Abraham
   Blussé (with J.C. Texier Westmuller, 1804-1810?)

Note: Edited by P.A. Antonelle
```

---

[13] In early serials, the function of an editor cannot be easily distinguished from the publisher, contributor, distributor, or financial investor in the serial. Named "authors" of early serials are usually the editors and/or principal contributors to the serial.

1E2. Statements of responsibility in other sources

If a statement of responsibility appears in a source other than the title page, or is taken from outside the serial, record the statement and its source in a note.

> *Note:* Edited by James Chalmers and his son, also James, who
>   assumed management of the Aberdeen journal at his father's
>   death in 1764; see Craig
>
> *Note:* Edited by John Dunton and Richard Wolley; see NCBEL
>
> *Note:* Author given in text of no. 1 as: "Fletcher, author and
>   preparer of the Royal antidote." Probably Richard Fletcher, who
>   wrote several works on medical remedies during the 1670s and
>   1680s
>
> *Note:* Editorship is sometimes attributed to Edward Rawlins (see
>   Nelson & Seccombe) or to Thomas Flatman (see Yale Library
>   catalog)

1E3. Transposition of statements of responsibility

If a statement of responsibility precedes the title proper in the source, transpose it to its required position unless it is a grammatically inseparable part of the title proper according to one or more of the conditions enumerated in 1B1.1. When transposing the statement of responsibility, do not use the mark of omission. Make a note indicating the transposition.

> General orders no. ... / Headquarters, Department of Arizona,
>   Prescott
> *Note:* Statement of responsibility transposed from head of title

1E4. Single statements of responsibility with two or more names

Transcribe a single statement of responsibility as such whether the two or more persons or corporate bodies named in it perform the same function or different functions.

> The spectator / by Addison, Steele, Parnell ...
>
> Annals of medicine, for the year ... : exhibiting a concise view
>   of the latest and most important discoveries in medicine and
>   medical philosophy / by Andrew Duncan, Sen., M.D. and Andrew
>   Duncan, Jun., M.D. ...

1E5. Omission of names in statements of responsibility

When a single statement of responsibility names more than one person or corporate body performing the same function or with the same degree of responsibility, transcribe all the names mentioned. *Optionally*, if the responsible persons or bodies named in a single statement are considered too numerous to list exhaustively, all after the third may be omitted. Indicate the omission by the mark of omission and supply "et al." in square brackets.

```
Journal hebdomadaire de médecine / par MM. Andral, Blandin,
    Bouilland ... [et al.]
```

1E6. Two or more statements of responsibility

If there are two or more statements of responsibility, transcribe them in the order indicated by their sequence on, or by the layout of, the title page. If the sequence and layout are ambiguous or insufficient to determine the order, transcribe the statements in the order that makes the most sense.

```
The comic almanack : an ephemeris in jest and earnest, containing
    merry tales, humorous poetry, quips, and oddities / by
    Thackeray, Albert Smith, Gilbert À Beckett, the brothers Mayhew
    ... ; with many hundred illustrations by George Cruikshank and
    other artists
```

1E7. Terms of address, etc., in statements of responsibility

Include titles and abbreviations of titles of nobility, address, honor, and distinction that appear with names in statements of responsibility.

```
/ by Dr. Silvester Partridge

/ by Sir Alexander Drawcansir, knt. (otherwise Henry Fielding,
    Esq.)

/ by the Rev. Mr. Bundy
```

1E8. Qualifications in statements of responsibility

Qualifications such as initials indicating membership in societies, academic degrees, and statements of positions held may be omitted from the statement of responsibility, using the mark of omission, unless:

the qualifications are necessary grammatically

or the qualifications are necessary for identifying the person or are useful in establishing a context for the person's activity (initials of religious orders, phrases, or adjectives denoting place names, etc.)

or   the statement of responsibility represents the author only by a pseudonym, a descriptive phrase, or nonalphabetic symbols.

1E9. Ambiguous statements of responsibility

If the relationship between the title of a work and the person(s) or body (bodies) named in the statement of responsibility is not clear, supply an explanatory word or short phrase in the language of the text, within square brackets, or make a note.

```
The rambler / by Samuel Johnson
Note: Of the 208 numbers all were by Johnson except: no. 10, by
    Hester Mulso, afterward Mrs. Chapone; no. 30, by Catharine
    Talbot; no. 97, by Samuel Richardson; no. 44 and 100, by
    Elizabeth Carter. Parts of no. 15 and 107 are by unknown
    correspondents
```

If considered important, make notes about expansions, explanations, and corrections of statements of responsibility when needed for clarity (see 7B6).

1E10. Statements of responsibility in more than one language or script

1E10.1. If there are titles in more than one language or script, but only a single statement of responsibility, transcribe the statement of responsibility after all the title information.

```
Current school enrolment statistics = Statistiques des effectifs
    scolaires / Unesco
```

1E10.2. If there are both titles and statements of responsibility in more than one language or script, transcribe each statement of responsibility after the title proper, parallel title, or other title information to which it relates. If any of these titles lack a matching statement of responsibility, transcribe the information in the order indicated by the sequence on, or by the layout of, the title page.

```
Opera, ballet, music-hall in the world / International Theatre
    Institute = Opéra, ballet, music-hall dans le monde / Institut
    international du théâtre
```

1E10.3. Make a note to indicate the original position in the source of any transposed statements.

1E11. Nouns and noun phrases

Treat a noun or noun phrase occurring in conjunction with a statement of responsibility as other title information if it is indicative of the nature of the work.

```
The busy body : a collection of periodical essays, moral,
    whimsical, comic, and sentimental / by Mr. Oulton
```

1E12. Persons or bodies not explicitly named in statements of responsibility

Transcribe a statement of responsibility as such even if no person or body is explicitly named in that statement. Such statements will generally contain words like "translated," "edited," "compiled," etc.

```
The historical and political mercury / translated from the French
```

1E13. Statements of responsibility with grammatically inseparable elements

If the statement of responsibility includes information belonging to another area, and the information is grammatically inseparable from the statement of responsibility according to one or more of the conditions enumerated in 1B1.1, transcribe it as part of the statement of responsibility.

```
The new weekly novelist, or, Entertaining companion : containing
    a new and complete collection of interesting romances and
    novels : a work designed for instruction as well as
    entertainment, being calculated to convey a general knowledge
    of the world ... : not to be found in any other work of the
    kind in English / the whole newly translated from the French,
    by Lewis Porney, Esq.
```

1E14. Phrases about notes, appendixes, etc.

1E14.1. Transcribe phrases about notes, appendixes, and such accompanying matter in the order indicated by the sequence on the title page. If such information appears before the statement of responsibility, transcribe it as other title information (see 1D3.1).

```
The guardian : in two volumes : to which is added, a translation
    of the mottos and quotations : together with the arguments, and
    writers names of such as are known, prefixed to each paper :
    not in any other edition
```

1E14.2. If such information appears after the statement of responsibility, transcribe it as a subsequent statement of responsibility, whether or not it names a person or body.

```
The idler / by Samuel Johnson, L.L.D. ; two volumes in one ; with
    additional essays ; to which is prefixed an account of the life
    and writings of the author
```

1E14.3. *Optionally*, if the phrases are very lengthy and can be abridged without loss of essential information, omit less important words or phrases, using the mark of omission. If considered important, transcribe omitted phrases in a note.

1E15. Change in statements of responsibility

If a person or body is added, changed, or deleted in a subsequent issue and this change does not require a new description (see Appendix E), give the name of the later person or body in a note or make a note of the change (see 7B6.7). If the change is only in the presentation of the name of the person or body, make a note if the change is considered to be important.

2. EDITION AREA

Contents:
2A.   Preliminary rule
2B.   Edition statement
2C.   Statements of responsibility relating to the edition
2D.   Statement relating to a named revision of an edition
2E.   Statements of responsibility relating to a named revision of an edition

2A. Preliminary rule

2A1. Prescribed punctuation

For instructions on the use of spaces before and after prescribed punctuation, see 0E.

Precede the edition area by a period-space-dash-space.

Precede a statement relating to a named revision of an edition by a comma.

Precede the first statement of responsibility following an edition statement by a diagonal slash.

Precede each subsequent statement of responsibility by a semicolon.

For the use of the equals sign to precede parallel statements, see the appropriate rules following.

2A2. Sources of information

The prescribed sources of information for the edition area are the title page, other preliminaries, colophon, and dust jacket (see introductory section IX.2), in that order of preference. If an edition statement or any part of the edition area is transcribed from elsewhere than the title page, indicate its source in a note.

2A3. Form and order of information

Transcribe edition information in the form and order in which it is presented in the source, unless instructed otherwise by specific rules (see 0G).

2B. Edition statement

2B1. General rule

Transcribe a statement relating to an edition as it appears if it pertains to the serial as a whole. Transcribe according to the general rules 0B-0G if the edition statement belongs to one of the following types.

a) local edition statements

```
Northern edition
```

b) special interest edition statements

```
Edition pour le medecin

Pony edition
```

c) special format or physical presentation statements

```
Library edition
```

d) language edition statements

```
English edition
```

e) reprint or reissue statements indicating a reissue or revision of the serial as a whole

```
Second edition

Revised edition

The sixth edition
```

2B2. Words considered part of the edition statement

2B2.1. Edition statements normally include either the word "edition" (or its equivalent in other languages), or a related term such as "revision" or "issue."

```
The second edition

Die dritte Aufflage

Fourth edition, revised and corrected

The second edition, corrected and greatly enlarg'd
```

2B2.2. Treat a phrase such as "newly printed" as an edition statement unless it is part of a statement being transcribed in the publication, distribution, etc., area. In case of doubt, treat such a statement as an edition statement.

```
Newly imprinted for all subscribers
```
> (*Comment:* But transcribe a statement such as "Philadelphia printed, London reprinted" in the publication, distribution, etc., area rather than the edition area)

2B2.3. Record statements indicating numbering in the numbering area (see 3B) unless the statement applies to the serial as a whole.

2B3. Edition statements with special characters or a numeric emphasis

2B3.1. If an edition statement consists entirely or chiefly of characters that are neither numeric nor alphabetic, transcribe the characters as they appear if the necessary typographical facilities are available. For characters that cannot be reproduced, substitute the names or descriptions of the characters in square brackets.

```
&&& edition

[Three stars] edition
```

2B3.2. If an edition statement consists of one or more letters or numbers without accompanying words, or only words that convey numbers, supply an appropriate word or abbreviation in square brackets. If no appropriate word or abbreviation can be determined, or in cases of doubt, simply transcribe the statement as found.

```
3e [éd.]

Second [ed.]
```

2B4. No edition statement

If the serial does not contain an edition statement, but is known to be a language, local, special interest, etc., edition, do not supply an edition statement based on this information. Give the information in a note.

```
Note: French edition of: The magazine of fantasy and science
   fiction

Note: Some vols. also called "American edition"

Note: English edition of the United States register, published in
   Philadelphia

Note: "Edinburgh edition"; see Nelson & Seccombe
```

2B5. Edition statements that are grammatically inseparable parts of other areas

If an edition statement is a grammatically inseparable part of another area according to one or more of the conditions enumerated in 1B1.1, and has been transcribed as such, do not repeat it as an edition statement.

```
Eclectic magazine and monthly edition of The living age
```

2B6. Transposition of edition statements

Transpose grammatically separable edition statements into the edition area from other parts of the title page. Provide details of the transposition in a note.

2B7. Edition statements in more than one language or script

2B7.1. If the serial bears edition statements in more than one language or script, transcribe the statement that is in the language or script of the title proper. If this criterion does not apply, transcribe the statement that appears first in the source. Transcribe the remaining statement(s), together with any associated statements of responsibility, as parallel edition statements. Precede each parallel statement by an equals sign. Make a note to indicate the original position in the source of any transposed statements.

2B7.2. *Optionally*, if it is considered that the parallel statements are too numerous to list exhaustively, and that some may be omitted without significant loss of identification, omit parallel statements after the first using the mark of omission. Transcribe the omitted statement(s) in a note, if considered important.

2B8. Variation in edition statement

2B8.1. If the edition statement varies or does not appear on all volumes or issues, ascertain whether the serial was issued as such (as opposed to being assembled from different editions). If the serial was issued as such, base the transcription on the first volume or issue and make a note to indicate variation in, or absence of, the edition statement in subsequent volumes or issues. In case of doubt, assume the serial was not issued as such.

```
Die dritte Aufflage
Note: Vol. 3- issued without the edition statement
```

2B8.2. If the serial is known or assumed to be a reissue assembled from different editions by a publisher, with a volume title page, consider the reissue to be a new serial (see Appendix J). Make a local note on variations in edition statements on individual issues, if considered important.

> *Local note:* No. 5: Third edition

2B8.3. If the serial is known or assumed to comprise issues assembled from different editions, without a volume title page, and reliable descriptions of the editions are available, make separate descriptions for each edition. In each description, make a local note indicating that the serial is incomplete and identifying which issue the description is based on and which issues are wanting.

2B8.4. If the serial is known or assumed to comprise issues assembled from different editions, without a volume title page, and reliable descriptions of the editions are not available, base the description on the copy in hand. Make a note to indicate that the description is based on issues assembled from different editions.

2B9. Change in edition statement

If an edition statement applying to the serial as a whole is added, deleted, or changed in a subsequent volume or issue, make a note if the change is considered important (see 7B8.5).

> American edition
> *Note:* No. 33-65: United States edition

2C. Statements of responsibility relating to the edition

2C1. General rule

2C1.1. Transcribe a statement of responsibility relating to one or more editions, but not to all editions, of a given work following the edition statement if there is one. Such statements may include the reviser or illustrator of a new edition, or a corporate body responsible for a new edition. Follow the instructions in 1E for the transcription and punctuation of such statements of responsibility.

> A new edition / corrected from the originals, with a preface,
>   historical and biographical, by Alex. Chalmers

2C1.2. Do not, however, apply this provision to such statements that do not name or otherwise identify a person or corporate body.

```
    The second edition revised and corrected

 not The second edition / revised and corrected
```

2C1.3. In determining the extent of the edition statement and the beginning of the statement of responsibility relating to the edition, it may be necessary to take into account the layout, punctuation, and typography of the title page as well as the sense of the text. Such words as "Revised and enlarged," when appearing with the name of a person or body, might be transcribed either as part of the edition statement or as part of the statement of responsibility relating to the edition, depending on their presentation on the title page.

2C2. Phrases about notes, appendixes, etc.

2C2.1. If there are phrases about notes, appendixes, and such supplementary matter and they apply to the edition in hand but not necessarily to all editions of the work, transcribe them as statements of responsibility relating to the edition only in the case when the phrase names or otherwise identifies a person or corporate body and appears in the same source as the edition statement.

```
    A corrected edition / with a preface, historical and
        biographical, by Alexander Chalmers
```

2C2.2. If the phrase does not name a person or corporate body, transcribe it as part of the edition statement proper or as part of the first statement of responsibility relating to the edition, as appropriate. Do not introduce the semicolon (as in 1E14.2) to separate such phrases from preceding statements of responsibility.

```
    A new edition illustrated with frontispieces

    The second edition, with compleat indexes ...
```

2C2.3. If such phrases have been transposed from a position preceding the edition statement, provide details of the transposition in a note.

2C3. Statements of responsibility relating to the edition in more than one language or script

2C3.1. If the serial has parallel edition statements (see 2B7) but a statement of responsibility relating to the edition in only one language or script, transcribe the statement of responsibility after all the edition statements.

2C3.2. If the serial has parallel edition statements (see 2B7) and statements of responsibility relating to the edition in more than one language or script, transcribe each statement of responsibility after the edition statement to which it relates.

2C3.3. Make a note to indicate the original position in the source of any transposed statements of responsibility.

2D. Statement relating to a named revision of an edition

If the serial is a named revision of an edition of an entire serial (a named reissue of a particular edition containing changes from that edition), transcribe the statement relating to that revision as instructed in 2B.

> ```
> English edition, Second edition
> ```
> (*Comment:* Statement indicates the serial is a revision of the first English edition)

2E. Statements of responsibility relating to a named revision of an edition

Transcribe a statement of responsibility relating to a named revision of an edition following the statement relating to the revision according to the applicable provisions of 2C.

3. NUMBERING AREA

Contents:

3A. Preliminary rule

3A1. Applicability

Give this area only if cataloging from the first and/or last volume or issue.

This area is not used for unnumbered monographic series.

3A2. Prescribed punctuation

For instructions on the use of spaces before and after prescribed punctuation, see 0E.

Precede this area by a period-space-dash-space.

Follow a numeric and/or alphabetic designation and/or the date of the first volume or issue of a serial by a hyphen.

Replace a hyphen with a forward slash for a span of numeric or chronological designations in a single volume or issue.

Enclose a date following a numeric and/or alphabetic designation in parentheses.

Precede an alternative numbering, etc., system by an equals sign when more than one system of designation is used.

Precede a new sequence of numbering, etc., by a semicolon.

3A3. Form and order of information

Transcribe numbering information in the form, but not necessarily with the same punctuation or in the same order, in which it is presented in the source, unless instructed otherwise by specific rules (see 0G). Do not abbreviate or expand words given in the designation. Transcribe numbering exactly as it appears in a note, if considered important.

```
Vol. I, no. XI (January 26, 1702/3 [i.e. 1703])-
```
Optional note: Dateline reads: No. XI January 26. 1702-3. Vol. I

3B. Numeric and/or alphabetic designation

3B1. Give the numeric and/or alphabetic designation of the first and/or last volume or issue of a serial as given on the volume or issue.

```
Premiere issue-

Number 1-number 6

First meeting-

Vol. I, first sess.-

Volume 1, no. 1-

-vol. V

Numb. I.-numb. XII

The first part-the sixth part

1st edition-

Der neuen Reihenfolge I-
```

3B2. If the sequence of numbering is continued from a previous serial, give the numbering of the first volume or issue of the serial represented by the new description. Make an explanatory note, if considered important.

```
Volume 5, no. 4-
```
Optional note: Numbering begins with v. 5, no. 4, continuing the numbering of the earlier title

3B3. If a numeric and/or alphabetic designation appears in more than one language or script, give the designation that is in the language or script of the title proper. If this criterion does not apply, give the designation that appears first.

3C. Chronological designation

3C1. If the first and/or last volume or issue of a serial is identified by a chronological designation, give it in the same terms, but not necessarily with the same punctuation used in the item. Do not abbreviate or expand words given in the designation.

```
1776-

April 1850-

Decemb. 18, 1775-

Issue for 1849-

-February 1800

January 1718-March 1719
```

3C2. If the chronological designation includes a date in roman numerals, transcribe the date as it appears. Omit internal spaces and punctuation (see 0G3.4, 0G4.1).

```
Année MDCCLXX-année MDCCLXXXVI
```

3C3. When the chronological designation is based on the Julian (Old Style) calendar, and the serial is known to have been issued in the following year according to the Gregorian (New Style) calendar (see 4D2.4), transcribe the date as it appears and supply the Gregorian year in square brackets. Make a note to indicate the basis of the supplied year. Do not amend the month and day, if present, by supplying Gregorian equivalents. In case of doubt, do not adjust the year.

```
January 27, 1641 [i.e. 1642]-
Note: Some issues dated according to Lady Day dating
```

3C4. If two dates appear in the designation, representing both Julian and Gregorian dating, transcribe both dates, separated by a slash. Supply the Gregorian year in square brackets, if necessary.

```
5th of Febr. 1701/02 [i.e. 1702]-

1690/1691 [i.e. 1691]-
```

3C5. If the chronological designation includes a date not of the Julian or Gregorian calendar, supply the corresponding date of the Julian or Gregorian calendar in square brackets.

```
1re décade de vendémiaire an VII [22 Sept.-1 Oct. 1798]-
```
    (*Comment:* Designation follows French Revolutionary calendar)

3C6. Enclose elements from outside sources in square brackets and indicate their source in a note.

```
[1793]-
Note: Date of first volume from Crane & Kaye
```

3C7. If a chronological designation appears in more than one language or script, give the designation that is in the language or script of the title proper. If this criterion does not apply, give the designation that appears first. Make a note giving the designations in each language, if considered important.

```
May 1977-
Optional note: Designation appears in English and French text
    (i.e. May 1977 and mai 1977)
```

```
not May 1977 = mai 1977-
```

3C8. If the first and/or last volume or issue of a serial is identified by both a numeric and/or alphabetic designation and a chronological designation, give the numeric and/or alphabetic designation before the chronological designation.

```
Num. 26 (Thursday, of the seventh week of the newe yeer, the
    eighth of May in the yeare of our Lord, 1644)-

Number 1 (Saturday, March 27, 1790)-

No. I (January 1788)-

Number I (for January 1783)-

Volume 2, no. 3 (June 1776)-

Number I (for the month of March, 1697)-

Numb. 1 (Thursday, October the 7 to Saturday, October the 9
    [1667])-
Note: Year from no. 2

Numb. I (Saturday, November 9, 1734)-

No 1er (mercredi, 7 mars 1764)-

Numb. 4 (dated at Sunderland, March 12, 1644)-

Numb. 1 (Thursday, May 12, 1709)-numb. 5 (Thursday, June 9, 1709)

-no 24 (29 mars 1791)
```

```
Numb. I (Friday, April 21, 1721)-numb. XV (Wednesday, May 24,
    1721)

-tome quarante-troisième (depuis l'année MDCCLXXVI, jusques &
    compris l'année MDCCLXXIX)
```

3D. No designation in first volume or issue

If the first volume or issue of a serial lacks a numeric, alphabetic, chronological, or other designation, but subsequent volumes or issues define a designation pattern, supply a numeric, alphabetic, chronological, etc., designation in square brackets, as appropriate, based on that pattern for the first volume or issue. If information about designations of subsequent volumes or issues is not available, give [No. 1]- (or its equivalent in the language of the title proper) or a chronological designation for the first volume or issue, as appropriate.

```
[No. 1]-
```
> (*Comment*: Subsequent issues numbered: No. 2, No. 3, etc.)

```
[Part 1]-
```
> (*Comment*: Subsequent issues numbered: Part 2, Part 3, etc.)

3E. Alternative numbering systems

If a serial has one or more alternative systems of designation that appear in the same source as the primary system of designation, record the systems in the order in which they are presented. If the alternative numbers are grammatically inseparable, transcribe them as they appear. Make a note about numbering appearing elsewhere, if considered important (see 7B9).

```
Vol. II, no. 6-  = 37th week since the beginning of publication-

Vol. 3, no. 4 (April 30, 1795)-vol. 4, no. 61 (November 15, 1796)
    = 212-272

Volume 73, no. 4 (Oct. 1987)-  = whole no. 437-

Erstes Stück, oder, ersten Bandes, erstes Stück-neuntes Stück,
    oder, zweiten Bandes, drittes Stück
```

3F. Change in numbering or designations

3F1. If the numbering starts a new sequence with a different system, transcribe the designation of the first and last volumes or issues under the old system, followed by the designation of the first volume or issue under the new system.

```
Numb. 1 (17th June 1761)-numb. 556 (30th April 1764) ; 2nd May
   1764-
```

3F2. If a new sequence is accompanied by wording to differentiate the sequence, such as "new series," transcribe this wording. Do not confuse such wording with that of a section title to be placed after a common title.

```
Vol. 12, no. 1-vol. 13, no. 4 ; new ser., vol. 1, no. 1-

December 1787-June 1825 ; new series, vol. I, no. I (September
   1825)-new series, vol. II, no. X (June 1826)
```

3F3. If a new sequence with the same system is not accompanied by wording such as "new series," supply "[new ser.]" or another appropriate term (or its equivalent in the language of the title proper). Use standard abbreviations found in AACR2 Appendix B.

```
1 (spring 1936)-5 (spring 1938) ; [new ser.], 1 (autumn 1938)-
   [new ser.], 3 (Christmas 1939)

-Nr. 146 (10 August 1790) ; [n.F.], Nr. 1 (17 August 1790)-

No 1 (1re décade de vendémiaire, an VII [22 Sept.-1 Oct. 1798])-
   no 36 (3e décade de fructidor, an VII [7-16 Sept. 1798]) ;
   [nouv. sér.], no 1 (1re décade de vendémiaire, an VIII [22
   Sept.-1 Oct. 1799])-[nouv. sér.], no 5 (2e décade de brumaire,
   an VIII [1-10 Nov. 1799])
```

3F4. Give a note for other variations in designations that do not constitute a new sequence if the change is considered important (see 7B9.2).

3G. Volume title page for collected issues or reissued serials

3G1. If a serial has a volume title page, give the designation that appears on the volume title page.

```
Vol. 1-

Vol. I-vol. VIII

Volume the first-volume the sixth

Tome premier (comprenant les mois de mars, avril & mai 1764)-tome
   huitieme (comprenant les mois de décembre 1765, janvier &
   février 1766)
```

3G2. If no designation appears on the volume title page or there is no volume title page, but designations appear on individual issues, give the designations that appear on the individual issues. Give the source of the designation in a note.

```
Numb. 1 (Tuesday, March 20, 1750)-numb. 34 (Saturday, July 14,
   1750)
Note: Designation taken from individual issues
```

3G3. If there are designations on both the volume title page and on the individual issues, give the designation that appears on the volume title page. Make a note recording the designations that appear on the individual issues. If it is not feasible to record designations of each volume, record designations of the first and/or last volumes.

```
Volume the first-volume the third
Note: Individual issues have designations: v. 1: Numb. I
   (Tuesday, November 7, 1752)-numb. XLVII (Tuesday, April 17,
   1753); v. 2: Numb. XLVIII (Saturday, April 21, 1753)-numb. XCII
   (Saturday, September 22, 1753); v. 3: Numb. XCIII (Tuesday,
   September 25, 1753)-numb. CXL (Saturday, March 9, 1754)

Tome premier (comprenant les mois de mars, avril & mai 1764)-tome
   huitieme (comprenant les mois de décembre 1765, janvier &
   février 1766)
Note: Individual issues have designations: v. 1: No 1er
   (mercredi, 7 mars 1764)-no 16 (mercredi, 6 juin 1764); v. 2: No
   17 (mercredi, 6 juin 1764)-no 32 (dimanche, 2 septembre 1764);
   v. 3: No 33 (mercredi, 5 septembre 1764)-no 48 (dimanche, 2
   décembre 1764); v. 4: No 49 (mercredi, 5 décembre 1764)-no 64
   (dimanche, 3 mars 1765); v. 5: No 1er (mercredi, 6 mars 1765)-
   no 12 (du 1r juin 1765); v. 6: No 13 (du 15 juin 1765)-no 18
   (du 1r septembre 1765); v. 7: No 19 (du 15 septembre 1765)-no
   23 (du 15 novembre 1765); v. 8: No 24 (du 1r décembre 1765)-no
   30 (du 1r mars 1766)

Vol. 1-
Note: Individual issues have designations: v. 1: Numb. 1 (April
   12, 1709)-numb. 109 (August 7, 1709)

Vol. I-vol. VIII
Note: Individual issues have designations: v. 1: No. 1 (Thursday,
   March 1, 1710-11)-no. 80 (Friday, June 1, 1711); v. 8: No. 556
   (Friday, June 18, 1714)-no. 635 (Monday, December 20, 1714)
```

3H. Misprints, etc., in the designation

If a number or date that is to be recorded as part of the designation is known to be incorrect, transcribe the incorrect form. Follow such an inaccuracy either by "[sic]" or by the abbreviation "i.e." and the correction within square brackets (see 0G7).

```
7th day of Feruary [sic], 1704 [i.e. 1740]-

#51 [i.e. 15] (Dec. 1, 1966)-
```

4. PUBLICATION, DISTRIBUTION, ETC., AREA

Contents:

4A. Preliminary rule

4A1. Prescribed punctuation

For instructions on the use of spaces before and after prescribed punctuation, see 0E.

Precede this area by a period-space-dash-space.

Precede a second or subsequently named place of publication, distribution, etc., by a semicolon, unless a linking word or phrase is given in the serial.

Precede the name of the first publisher, distributor, etc., by a colon. Precede the name of a second and any subsequent publisher, distributor, etc., by a colon, unless a linking word or phrase is given in the serial.

Precede the date of publication, distribution, etc., by a comma.

Enclose the details of manufacture (place, name, date) within parentheses.

Precede a second or subsequently named place of manufacture by a semicolon, unless a linking word or phrase is given in the serial.

Precede the name of the first manufacturer by a colon. Precede the name of a second and any subsequent manufacturer by a colon, unless a linking word or phrase is given in the serial.

Precede the date of manufacture by a comma.

For the use of the equals sign to precede parallel statements, see the appropriate rules following.

4A2. Sources of information

4A2.1. The prescribed source of information for the publication, distribution, etc., area is the whole serial. If statements belonging to different elements are found in separate sources, combine them to make a complete statement in the publication, distribution, etc., area. However, do not combine statements belonging to a single element when they appear in different sources within the serial.

4A2.2. If any part of the publication, distribution, etc., area is taken from a source other than the title page, make a note to indicate the source (see 7B10.1). Make a note about information not transcribed in the publication, distribution, etc., area, if considered important.

4A3. Form and order of information

4A3.1. Transcribe publication, distribution, etc., information in the form and order in which it is presented in the source, unless instructed otherwise by specific rules (see 0G).

4A3.2. If statements belonging to different elements appear out of order, or as part of another area, and they are grammatically separable, transpose them as needed. Make a note indicating the original position of the transposed elements.

```
New-York : Printed by J.S. Mott, for the editor, and C. Smith,
    no. 51 Maiden-Lane, Saturday, October 7, 1797
Note: Date follows place of publication in imprint
```

4A3.3. If the elements are not grammatically separable, or their transposition would result in an ambiguous or otherwise confusing construction, transcribe them in the order found and supply missing elements in square brackets as needed (see 0G6).

4A4. Fictitious or incorrect information

If all information relating to the publication, distribution, etc., area appearing in the serial is known to be fictitious or incorrect, transcribe it nonetheless. If the real details are known, or can be reasonably surmised, supply them at the end of the area as a correction in square brackets. Give the source of this information in a note. If some but not all of the information is known to be fictitious or incorrect, apply the appropriate rule (see 4B9, 4C5, 4D2.3).

```
[S.l.] : Printed in the world in the moon for J.J. to delight all
   the mad merry people under the sun, [1659] [i.e. London :
   Published by John Crouch]
Note: Correct imprint information from: Nelson & Seccombe, no.
   323
```

```
A Londres : Chez Golden Heat, an 1000 [i.e. Berlin : s.n., 1763]
Note: Corrected imprint from: British Library
```

4A5. Information covered by labels, etc.

If any of the original details relating to the publication, distribution, etc., area are covered by a label or other means showing later information, transcribe the later information. If the original details are visible or otherwise available, transcribe or give them in a note.

4A6. Elements relating to publication, distribution, etc., vs. elements relating to manufacture

Consider the wording, layout, and typography of the serial itself when determining the most appropriate place to transcribe information relating to the publication, distribution, etc., area. Keep in mind that statements relating to printing will sometimes be more appropriately transcribed as elements of publication, distribution, etc., and sometimes as elements of manufacture.[14] Consult the following instructions for guidance.

4A6.1. Statements relating to publication, distribution, etc., only. If the serial bears only a statement relating to publication, distribution, etc., or multiple such statements, transcribe the statement(s) according to the instructions in 4B, 4C, and 4D.

```
Forest Grove, Or. : Ind. Industrial School, 1884-
```

---

[14] The roles of publishers, printers, and booksellers were not clearly delimited in the hand-press period. Statements relating to printing frequently appear prominently on early printed materials, reflecting the tendency of printers to function as more than solely manufacturers. As the book trade industry became increasingly specialized over time, however, the role of the publisher gradually assumed greater importance, while the roles of manufacturer and distributor came to be subordinate.

```
London : Printed by J.D. and are to be sold by Tho. Corbett, 1714

[Aberdeen, Scotland] : Printed and sold by James Chalmers, and by
   Alexander Thomson bookseller, [1748-1768]
```

4A6.2. Statements relating to manufacture only

4A6.2.1. If the serial bears only a statement relating to manufacture, or multiple such statements, generally assume the manufacturer(s) to also be functioning as publisher(s), distributor(s), etc. Transcribe the statement(s) according to the instructions in 4B, 4C, and 4D. Consider the words "place of publication" and "publisher" in those instructions to refer equally to the place of manufacture and name of manufacturer in such cases.

```
Chelmsford : Printed by T. Toft and R. Lobb, 1764-1771

Edmonton : Jas. E. Richards, government printer, 1907

A Jersey [Saint Helier, Channel Islands] : De l'imprimerie de
   Math. Alexandre, 1786-

Albany : Printed by Websters and Skinners ; New-York :
   Stereotyped by G. Bruce, 1822
```

4A6.2.2. However, if the manufacturer is known not to be the publisher, distributor, etc., and the identity of the publisher, distributor, etc., can be determined or reasonably surmised, supply the name of the publisher, distributor, etc., in square brackets and transcribe the manufacturer statement as such according to the instructions in 4E, 4F, and 4G.

```
[Boston : New York & Erie Railroad Company, 1856] (Boston :
   Farwells & Forrest, steam job printers, 5 Lindall Street)
```

4A6.3. Statements relating both to publication, distribution, etc., and to manufacture

If the serial bears statements relating both to publication, distribution, etc., and to manufacture, determine whether or not the statements are grammatically separable.

4A6.3.1. If the statements are grammatically inseparable, transcribe them according to the instructions in 4B, 4C, and 4D. Consider the words "place of publication" and "publisher" in those instructions to refer equally to the place of manufacture and name of manufacturer in such cases.

```
West-Chester [Pa.] : Printed by Derrick and Sharples, and sold by
   the principal booksellers in Philadelphia, 1797

[Aberdeen, Scotland] : Printed and sold by James Chalmers, and by
   Alexander Thomson bookseller, [1748-1768]

London : Printed by J.D. and are to be sold by Tho. Corbett, 1714
```

4A6.3.2. If the statements are grammatically separable, determine which statement is emphasized in the source, whether typographically (larger font size, uppercase letters, boldface, etc.) or by appearing first in sequence in the source.

4A6.3.2.1. If a manufacturer statement has been emphasized, transcribe all of the statements according to the instructions in 4B, 4C, and 4D. Consider the words "place of publication" and "publisher" in those instructions to refer equally to the place of manufacture and name of manufacturer in such cases.

```
London : Printed for J. How, in Talbot-Court, in Grace Church
   Street, and G. Sawbridge, in Little-Britain, and sold at the
   Publishing-Office, in Bearbinder-Lane, 1707-1708

Amstelaedami : Apud Janssonio-Waesbergios, 1740-1751

London : Printed by C. Ackers in St. John's Street, for J.
   Wilford, behind the Chapter-House in St. Paul's Church-Yard, T.
   Cox [sic] at the Lamb under the Royal-Exchange. J. Clarke at
   the Golden-Ball in Duck-Lane, and T. Astley at the Rose over-
   against the North Door of St. Pauls, [1732-1735]

London : Printed for S. Crowder, in Pater-noster-Row, J. Wilkie,
   no. 71, St. Paul's Church yard, and J. Walter, at Charing
   Cross, -MDCCLXXII [1772]
```

4A6.3.2.2. If a publisher, distributor, etc., statement has been emphasized, transcribe the publisher, distributor, etc., statement(s) according to the instructions in 4B, 4C, and 4D and transcribe the manufacturer statement(s) according to the instructions in 4E, 4F, and 4G.

```
[S.l.] : Philalethes [i.e. Charles Leslie], 1708 (London :
   Printed and sold by the booksellers of London and Westminster)
```

4B. Place of publication, distribution, etc.

4B1. General rule

4B1.1. Transcribe the names of places associated with publishers, distributors, and booksellers as part of this element. Transcribe the names of places associated with printers and other manufacturers only if appropriate according to the instructions in 4A6 (i.e., when the wording, layout, or typography of the serial suggests that the manufacturer is also functioning as the publisher, distributor, etc.).

4B1.2. Transcribe the place of publication, distribution, etc., as it appears in the source. If the place appears together with the name of a larger jurisdiction (e.g., country, state, or similar designation), or multiple such jurisdictions, transcribe this as well.

```
Elizabeth-Town

Köln

Commonwealth of Massachusetts, Boston

Saskatoon, Saskatchewan, Canada

San Francisco, Cal.

Bruxelles, Belgique
```

4B2. Places of publication, distribution, etc., with initial prepositions, etc.

Include in the transcription any prepositions appearing before the place of publication, distribution, etc., as well as any accompanying words or phrases associated with the place name.

```
A Paris

In London

In Boston, printed
```
> (*Comment:* Title page reads: "In Boston, printed. 1705." Following provisions of 4D1.3, "printed" is here transcribed with the place)

```
Printed at Bennington
```

4B3. Supplied modern forms of place names

If considered necessary for identification and if known, supply in square brackets the modern form of the name of the place. Use an English form of the name, if there is one.

```
Christiania [Oslo]

Lerpwl [Liverpool]
```

```
Berolini [Berlin]
```

4B4. Supplied fuller forms of place names

If a place name is found only in an abbreviated form in the source, transcribe it as found. Supply in square brackets the full form of the name, or the remainder of the name, if considered necessary for identification.

```
Mpls [i.e. Minneapolis]

Rio [de Janeiro]
```

4B5. Supplied larger jurisdictions

Supply in square brackets the name of the country, state, province, etc., after the name of the place if it is considered necessary for identification, or if it is considered necessary to distinguish the place from others of the same name. Use a modern English form of the name, if there is one. Apply the abbreviations appearing in AACR2, Appendix B.

```
Cambridge [England]

Newport [R.I.]

Washington [Pa.]
```

4B6. Two or more places of publication, distribution, etc.

4B6.1. If the source of information shows two or more places and all are related to the same publisher, transcribe all in the order in which they appear.

```
London ; York

A Lausanne & se trouve à Paris
```

4B6.2. *Optionally,* if it is considered that the places are too numerous to list exhaustively, and that some may be omitted without significant loss of identification, the place of publication, distribution, etc., statement may be shortened by omitting all the places after the third. In such cases, use the mark of omission and supply after it in square brackets a phrase in the language and script of the cataloging agency to convey the extent of the omission. Include the number of omitted places (if more than one) in the supplied phrase.

```
London ; Salisbury ; Winchester ... [and 10 provincial towns]
```

4B6.3. If a subsequent place of publication, distribution, etc., is not related to the same publisher, transcribe it in association with the publisher, distributor, etc., to which it corresponds.

```
Philadelphia : Published by Moore & Waterhouse, no. 45 North
    Sixth Street ; Pittsburgh, Pa. : John Libby, 1837-
    ([Philadelphia] : J. Van Court, printer, corner of Bread and
    Quarry St. rear of 96 N. Second)
Note: Printer from colophon
```

4B6.4. Do not, however, transcribe a subsequent place as a place of publication, distribution, etc., if it must be recorded as a grammatically inseparable part of another element.

```
Printed at Worcester, Massachusetts : By Isaiah Thomas : Sold by
    him in Worcester, by said Thomas and Andrews in Boston, and by
    said Thomas and Carlisle, in Walpole, Newhampshire
```

4B6.5. If a place of publication, distribution, etc., associated with an earlier edition appears together with the actual place of publication, distribution, etc., of the edition being described, transcribe the places as a single element in the order in which they appear.

```
Philadelphia printed, London reprinted
```

4B6.6. If both the place and publisher, distributor, etc., associated with an earlier edition appear together with the place and publisher, distributor, etc., of the edition being described, transcribe each place with the publisher, distributor, etc., to which it corresponds.

```
Kaskaskia : Printed by Matthew Duncan, printer to the territory ;
    Springfield : Reprinted by Phillips Bros., state printers
```

4B7. Change in place of publication, distribution, etc.

4B7.1. If the place of publication, distribution, etc., changes in a subsequent volume or issue, give the later place(s) in a note.

```
Douglas, Arizona
Note: Place of publication varies: Issue 2-  Bisbee, Arizona
```

4B7.2. *Optionally*, if the changes are numerous, a general statement may be made.

```
Note: Place of publication varies
```

4B8. Place names that are grammatically inseparable parts of other areas, etc.

If the place of publication, distribution, etc., appears only as a grammatically inseparable part of another area and is transcribed there, or appears only as a grammatically inseparable part of the publisher, distributor, etc., statement and is transcribed there, supply in square brackets the place of publication, distribution, etc., as the first element of the publication, distribution, etc., area (see 4C3). Use a modern English form of the name, if there is one.

```
[London] : Printed also in the French tongue, for the author
    James Whiston, moderatour to merchants, living in Water-lane by
    the Custom-House, London, who delivers either of them weekly
    every Monday where desired for twenty shillings per annum

[Munich] : Durch Peter Clement, Kunstführer zu München
```

4B9. Fictitious or incorrect places of publication, distribution, etc.

If the place of publication, distribution, etc., appearing in the serial is known to be fictitious or incorrect, supply a correction in square brackets, using a modern English form of name, if there is one, and give the basis for the correction in a note. If, however, the entire statement consisting of place, publisher, and date is known to be fictitious or incorrect, apply 4A4.

```
Londres [i.e. Paris]
Note: Actual place of publication from: Nelson & Seccombe
```

4B10. No place of publication, distribution, etc.

4B10.1. If no place of publication, distribution, etc., appears in the serial, supply one in square brackets. Use a modern English form of the name, if there is one, and include the name of the larger jurisdiction if considered necessary for identification. Use the location associated with the first transcribed publisher, distributor, etc., if one is present. Provide a justification for the supplied place in a note if necessary.

```
[Cambridge, Mass.] : Printed by Samuel Green, 1668-
Note: Samuel Green was located in Cambridge, Mass., from 1660 to
    1672
```

4B10.2. If the name of the place has changed over time, supply the name appropriate to the date of publication, distribution, etc., if known (e.g., Leningrad, not St. Petersburg, for works published in that city between 1924 and

1991). If considered necessary for identification, also supply the modern place name and the name of the larger jurisdiction.

```
[Christiania i.e. Oslo]

[Leona Vicario i.e. Saltillo, Coahuila, Mexico]
```

4B11. Place of publication, distribution, etc., supplied based on address or sign

Supply in square brackets the name of the place of publication, distribution, etc., using a modern English form of the name, if there is one, when only an address or sign appears in the serial. (Transcribe the address or sign as the publisher, distributor, etc., statement; see 4C4.1.) When supplying the place, give a justification in a note if necessary.

```
[Paris]
```
> (*Comment:* Imprint reads: "à l'enseigne de l'éléphant," the trade sign of a Parisian printer)

```
[London]
```
> (*Comment:* Imprint reads: "sold in St. Paul's Church Yard")

4B12. Place of publication, distribution, etc., uncertain or unknown

4B12.1. If the place of publication, distribution, etc., is uncertain, supply the name of the probable place of publication, distribution, etc., with a question mark, using a modern English form of the name, if there is one, all in square brackets.

```
[Amsterdam?]

[Newport, R.I.?]

[St. Petersburg?]
```

4B12.2. If no city of publication, distribution, etc., can be conjectured, supply the name of a state, province, country, or other larger geographic entity as the place of publication, distribution, etc., with a question mark if necessary, using a modern English form of the name, if there is one, all in square brackets.

```
[Canada]

[Surrey?]

[South America?]
```

4B12.3. If the reason for supplying the place is not apparent from the rest of the description, make a note to indicate the source of the information.

> *Note:* Place of publication from Nelson & Seccombe

4B12.4. If no place of publication, distribution, etc., can be supplied, use the abbreviation "s.l." (sine loco) in square brackets.

> [S.l.]

4B13. Place names in more than one language or script

4B13.1. If the name of the place of publication, distribution, etc., appears in more than one language or script, transcribe the statement in the language or script of the title proper, or if this criterion does not apply, transcribe the statement that appears first in sequence in the source. Transcribe the remaining statement(s) as parallel statements, preceding each by an equals sign. Make a note to indicate the original position in the source of any transposed statements.

4B13.2. *Optionally*, if it is considered that the parallel statements are too numerous to list exhaustively, and that some may be omitted without significant loss of identification, omit parallel statements after the first using the mark of omission. Transcribe the omitted statement(s) in a note, if considered important.

4C. Name of publisher, distributor, etc.

4C1. Transcribe the names of publishers, distributors, and booksellers as part of this element. Transcribe the names of printers and other manufacturers only if appropriate according to the instructions in 4A6 (i.e., when the wording, layout, or typography of the serial suggests that the manufacturer is also functioning as the publisher, distributor, etc.).

4C2. Transcribe the name of the publisher, together with any associated words or phrases, as it appears in the serial.

> : Printed for J. Warner
>
> : Printed, and re-printed by E. Waters
>
> : Imprimerie d'E. Duverger, rue de Verneuil, no 4
>
> : Printed every Monday and Thursday, by Gillet and Co., no. 1412, rue Notre dame des champs, where all orders relative to this

```
paper are received : Published by M. Gueffier, bookseller, Quai
des Augustins
```

Optionally, omit addresses and insignificant information in the middle or at the end of the publisher, distributor, etc., statement, unless the information aids in identifying or dating the serial or is deemed important to the cataloging agency (e.g., for the purpose of capturing book trade data). Indicate all omissions by the mark of omission.

```
: Chez Testu, imprimeur-libraire ... Blanchon, libraire ... et
les marchands de nouveautés
```

```
: Printed for Ric. Chiswell ...
```

If a statement such as "Privately printed" appears on the title page, transcribe it as, or as part of, the publisher, distributor, etc., statement.

```
: Privately printed
```

4C3. Publisher, distributor, etc., statements containing grammatically inseparable place names or dates

If the publisher, distributor, etc., statement contains grammatically inseparable statements relating to place or date of publication, distribution, etc., transcribe the information as part of the publisher, distributor, etc., element. Supply the place or date of publication, distribution, etc., in square brackets in the appropriate element (see 4B8, 4D1.8; see also 4A3.3).

```
[Berlin] : Verlag der Vereins-Buchhandlung in Berlin
```

4C4. Publisher, distributor, etc., statements containing only addresses, signs, or initials

4C4.1. If only the address, sign, or initials of the publisher, distributor, etc., appear in lieu of the name, transcribe the statement containing the address, sign, or initials as the publisher, distributor, etc., statement (see also 4B11). If the publisher's, distributor's, etc., name can be identified, supply it in square brackets after the initials or before or after the address or sign, as appropriate, or give the information in a note.

```
: Printed for W.W. [i.e. William Welby] and are to be solde in
  Paule's Church yarde at the signe of the Grey-hound
Note: Bookseller's name identified in STC (2nd ed.)
```

```
: Printed for I.T.
Note: Printed by Miles Flesher for John Trundle; see STC (2nd
   ed.)

: [Jean-Pierre Costard] rue Saint-Jean-de-Beauvais, la premiere
   porte cochere au dessus du College
Note: Costard listed as printer in Quérard

: Ad insigne Pinus [i.e. Hans Schultes, the Elder]

: Printed by T.F. for Nicholas Bourne
Note: T.F. is Thomas Forcet?
```

4C4.2. If the identification of the publisher, distributor, etc., is based on a device, supply the name of the publisher, distributor, etc., in square brackets, even if the device includes the publisher's initials or spelled-out name. Make notes as necessary about the basis for the identification, the source of the information used, the presence of the device, etc.

```
Printed at London [i.e. Edinburgh] : [Robert Bryson]
Note: Robert Bryson's device on t.p.; see Nelson & Seccombe
```

4C5. Fictitious or incorrect publisher, distributor, etc., statements

If the publisher, distributor, etc., statement is known to be fictitious or incorrect, supply a correction in square brackets and give the basis for the correction in a note. If, however, the entire statement consisting of place, publisher (distributor, etc.), and date is fictitious or incorrect, apply 4A4.

```
: Printed by A. Merryman [i.e. Abraham Ilive?], and sold by the
   hawkers
Note: Printer's name is probably a pseudonym; possibly Abraham
   Ilive (see Wiles, R.M.  Serial publication in England, p. 44-
   53)
```

4C6. Two or more names of publishers, distributors, etc.

4C6.1. If the publisher, distributor, etc., statement includes more than one publisher, distributor, etc., in a single source, transcribe all the names in the order in which they appear. Transcribe them as subsequent statements of publication, distribution, etc., only when they are not linked by connecting words or phrases.

```
: Printed for J. Newbery, T. Becket, T. Davies, W. Jackson, in
   Oxford, and A. Kincaid, and Company, in Edinburgh
```

```
: In gemeinschaftlichem Verlag von Berenberg in Lauenburg und der
  Jaegerschen Buchhandl. in Frankfurt am Main
```

4C6.2. *Optionally*, if it is considered that the names are too numerous to list exhaustively, and that some may be omitted without significant loss of identification, the publisher, distributor, etc., statement may be shortened by omitting all the names after the third. In such cases, use the mark of omission and supply after it in square brackets a phrase in the language and script of the cataloging agency to convey the extent of the omission. Include the number of omitted publishers (or firms) and the number of omitted places (if more than one) in the supplied phrase.

```
: Printed for F.C. and J. Rivington, Otridge and Son, J. Nichols
  and Co. ... [and 26 others]

: Printed and sold by J. Newbery and C. Micklewright, also by
  Mess. Ware, Birt, Astley, Austen, Robinson, Dodsley, and
  Needham, in London ...[and 8 others in 8 other places]
```

4C7. Change in name of publisher, distributor, etc.

4C7.1. If the name or form of name of the publisher, distributor, etc., changes in a subsequent volume or issue, give the later name(s) in a note.

```
: Zero Press
Note: Publisher varies: Alphabet Press, summer 1949-winter 1950

: Printed for the profit of the seller, and the pleasure of the
  buyer
Note: Imprint varies; later issues list A. Purslow, A.P., or T.H.
  as printers, "for the general assembly of Hawkers"

: Sold by Langley Curtis
Note: Imprint varies; later issues list Anne Thompson as
  bookseller, and Brabazon Aylmer, John Walthoe, and Joseph Raven
  as publishers; some issues lack colophon
```

4C7.2. *Optionally*, if there are numerous minor changes in publisher, distributor, etc., a general statement may be made.

```
Publisher varies
```

4C8. Supplied and conjectured names of publishers, distributors, etc.

If no name, address, or device of a publisher, distributor, etc., appears in the serial, supply the name of the publisher, distributor, etc., in square brackets if known. If the responsibility of a publisher, distributor, etc., for a particular serial is conjectured, either add a question mark to any supplied name or give the information in a note. In any case of a supplied publisher, distributor, etc., give supporting evidence in a note.

```
[Dublin, Ireland : Printed by Walter Cox]
Note: Lacks imprint; place of publication and name of printer
   from Ingliss
```

4C9. No supplied name of publisher, distributor, etc.

If no publisher, distributor, etc., statement can be supplied, use the abbreviation "s.n." (sine nomine) in square brackets.

```
Paris : [s.n.]

[S.l. : s.n.]
```

4C10. Publisher, distributor, etc., transcribed as part of another area

If the name of the publisher, distributor, etc., does not appear in the publisher, distributor, etc., statement, but has already been transcribed as part of another area, supply it in a short identifiable form within square brackets.

```
Printed at my [i.e. Sam. Farley's] house near the New-Inn
```
        (*Comment:* Title reads: Sam. Farley's Exeter post-man, or, Weekly intelligence)

If transcribing a publisher, distributor, etc., statement in the publication, distribution, etc., area, however, do not abridge or expand the statement simply because it repeats or omits information given elsewhere in the description.

4C11. Publisher, distributor, etc., statements in more than one language or script

4C11.1. If the name of the publisher, distributor, etc., appears in more than one language or script, transcribe the statement in the language or script of the title proper, or if this criterion does not apply, transcribe the statement that appears first. Transcribe the remaining statement(s) as parallel statements, preceding each by an equals sign. Make a note to indicate the original position in the source of any transposed statements.

4C11.2. *Optionally,* if it is considered that the parallel statements are too numerous to list exhaustively, and that some may be omitted without significant loss of identification, omit parallel statements after the first using the mark of omission. Transcribe the omitted statement(s) in a note, if considered important.

4D. Date of publication, distribution, etc.

4D1. General rule

4D1.1. Transcribe dates of publication, distribution, etc., of the first and/or last volume or issue as part of this element. Transcribe dates of printing or other manufacture only if appropriate according to the instructions in 4A6 (i.e., when the wording, layout, or typography of the serial suggests that the manufacturer is also functioning as the publisher, distributor, etc.). Do not transcribe chronological designations as part of this element (see 3C).

4D1.2. Transcribe dates as they appear in the serial, including the day and month, if present.

4D1.3. Transcribe words and phrases such as "in the year" and "anno" as part of this element. If both the place and the date of printing appear in conjunction with the phrase "printed in the year," determine whether "printed" is to be transcribed with the place or the date according to the punctuation or typography of the source.

```
London printed : [s.n.], in the year 1742
```
> (*Comment:* Imprint reads: "London printed, in the year 1742")

```
London : [s.n.], printed in the year 1742
```
> (*Comment:* Imprint reads: "London, printed in the year 1742")

4D1.4. If the first volume or issue of the serial is available, record the beginning date followed by a hyphen.

```
, 1766-
```

```
, 7th July 1766-
```

```
, 1732, reprinted 1734-
```

4D1.5. If the serial has ceased and the first and last volumes or issues are available, record the beginning and ending dates, separated by a hyphen.

```
, 1766-1768
```

4D1.6. If the serial has ceased and the last volume or issue is available, but not the first, record the ending date, preceded by a hyphen.

```
, -1768
```

4D1.7. If both first and last volumes or issues are published in the same year, give the year only once.

```
, 1780
```

4D1.8. If the date is grammatically inseparable from information transcribed as part of another element or area according to one or more of the conditions enumerated in 1B1.1, transcribe it within that area or element and supply the date in square brackets as the date of publication.

4D2. Transcription involving adjustments or additions

4D2.1. Roman numerals. If the date appears in roman numerals, transcribe the date as it appears. Omit internal spaces and punctuation (see 0G3.4, 0G4.1). Supply the year(s) in arabic numerals in square brackets.

```
, anno domini MDCLIV [1654]-
```

```
, MDCCXXXVI-MDCCLXXXVI [1736-1786]
```
    (*Comment*: On first and last volumes: "M. DCCXXXVI." and "M. DCCLXXXVI.")

```
, 1716-MDCCXIX [1719]
```
    (*Comment:* Imprint in first volume has year in arabic numerals, later volumes in roman numerals)

4D2.2. Chronograms. If the date appears only in the form of a chronogram, substitute for it the date in arabic numerals in square brackets. If the supplied date includes a day/month, use the sequence: day, month, year. Make a note explaining the source of the date. Include a transcription of the original chronogram in the note, if considered important.

```
, [1740]
```
Optional note: Date of publication derived from chronogram: Ipso anno tertIo saeCVLarI typographIae DIVIno aVXILIo a gerManIs InVentae

```
, [8 Mar. 1643]
```
Note: Date of publication derived from chronogram in colophon

4D2.3. Fictitious or incorrect dates. If the year of publication, distribution, etc., is known to be fictitious or incorrect, transcribe it as it appears and supply the real or correct year in square brackets. If, however, the entire statement consisting of place, publisher (distributor, etc.), and date is fictitious or incorrect, apply 4A4.

```
, 1703 [i.e. 1730]-
```

If a date from the title page has been transcribed as the publication, distribution, etc., date, and evidence for a later date of publication, distribution, etc., appears in a source other than the title page, supply the later date in square brackets as a correction. If necessary, make a note to clarify that the date added as a correction is a differing date of publication, not a correction of an error on the title page.

```
, 1786 [i.e. 1788]-
Note: Dedication and preface of first issue both dated 1788
```

4D2.4. Julian/Old Style dates. If the year of publication, distribution, etc., is based on the Julian calendar (sometimes called the Old Style calendar) and the serial is known to have been published in the following year according to the Gregorian (New Style) calendar, transcribe the date as it appears and supply the Gregorian year in square brackets.[15] Make a note to indicate the basis for the supplied year. Do not amend the month and day, if present, by supplying Gregorian equivalents. In case of doubt, do not adjust the year.

```
, 1625 [i.e. 1626]-
```

If two dates appear in the serial, representing both Julian and Gregorian dating, transcribe both dates, separated by a slash. Supply the Gregorian year in square brackets, if necessary.

```
, 1690/1 [i.e. 1691]-
```

```
, 1690/1691 [i.e. 1691]-
```

4D2.5. Dates not of the Julian or Gregorian calendar. If the date of publication, distribution, etc., is based on a calendar other than the Julian or Gregorian

---

[15] The Julian calendar was gradually abandoned in favor of the Gregorian calendar beginning in 1582, with different countries adopting the calendar in different years. The difficulty in determining dates during this period is further complicated by the fact that January 1 was not universally used to reckon the start of a new year (e.g., before adopting the Gregorian calendar, Great Britain and its colonies long calculated the turn of the year on March 25, the Feast of the Annunciation or "Lady Day"). For assistance in establishing Gregorian dates, consult a reference source such as Adriano Cappelli's *Cronologia, Cronografia e Calendario Perpetuo* or C.R. Cheney's *Handbook of Dates for Students of English History*.

calendar, transcribe the date and supply the equivalent Julian or Gregorian year(s) in square brackets.

```
, an 5-an 8 [1797-1799]
```
    (*Comment:* Years follow French Revolutionary calendar)

4D2.6. Multiple adjustments or additions. If the date of publication, distribution, etc., requires more than a single adjustment or addition, provide all the supplied information within the same set of square brackets.

```
, MDCXIII [1613 i.e. 1693]-
Note: Corrected imprint date from Nelson & Seccombe

, anno MDCXLVIII [1648 i.e. 1649]-
Note: Imprint from colophon. Date of publication given in Old
   Style; see Nelson & Seccombe

, [620 i.e. 1859 or 1860]-
Note: Date of publication derived from chronogram on t.p.
```

4D3. Date of publication, distribution, etc., supplied from reference sources

If the date of publication, distribution, etc., does not appear in the serial but is known, supply it in square brackets from any source, preferably a reliable bibliography or reference work. Give the source of the supplied date(s) and any needed explanation in a note.

```
, [1676]-
Note: Publication date from NCBEL
```

4D4. Conjectural date of publication, distribution, etc.

4D4.1. If the first and/or last volumes or issues lack a date of publication, distribution, etc., dates from the designation, the text, or another part of the serial may be used as the basis of a supplied date of publication, distribution, etc. In these cases, give the date in arabic numerals in square brackets, with a question mark if necessary, and make a note on the source of the date. If dates are embedded in another part of the publication, distribution, etc., area, repeat the date in arabic numerals at the end, in square brackets.

```
, [1739-1748]
Note: Years of publication from chronological designations of
   volumes
```

```
, [1687]-
Note: Years of publication from chronological designations of
   issues

, [1641-1643]
Note: Years of publication from dates of coverage

, [1660?]
Note: Probable date from text

: Printed in May 1649, and are to be sold for the good of the
   state, [1649]-
```

4D4.2. If the first and/or last volume or issue is not available, supply the beginning or ending date with a question mark within square brackets in the publication, distribution, etc., area if it can be readily ascertained.

```
, [1789?]-
        (Comment: Earliest issue available is v. I, no. 3, 15 Oct. 1789, published weekly)
```

4D4.3. If the first and/or last volumes or issues of a serial are not available, and dates of publication, distribution, etc., cannot be readily ascertained or are not known, leave the element blank. *Optionally*, give the range of known dates in angle brackets. Give the source of the supplied date(s) and any needed explanation in a note.

```
, <1644>
Note: Only extant issue; see Nelson & Seccombe

, <1696-1716>
Note: Earliest known extant issue is no. 23, Aug. 13, 1696, and
   the latest, Dec. 22, 1716
```

4D5. Copyright dates and dates of deposit

4D5.1. Do not transcribe a copyright date or a date of deposit in the publication, distribution, etc., area.

4D5.2. If a date of publication, distribution, etc., does not appear in the source and it is likely that the date of copyright or deposit represents the date of publication, distribution, etc., supply the date in square brackets as the date of publication. Include a question mark if the supplied date is conjectural. Make a note to indicate that the basis for the supplied date is the date of copyright or deposit. Include in the note as much information as is deemed important to the cataloging agency. If transcribing a copyright symbol in the note, use a lowercase c to represent the symbol if it cannot be reproduced using available typographic facilities.

```
, [1880?]-
Note: Copyright statement dated 1880 on t.p. verso of first issue

, [1866?]-
Note: "Entered, according to Act of Congress, in the year 1866
    ... in the clerk's office of the Dist. Court of the U.S., for
    the Southern District of New York"--No. 1, t.p. verso

, [1976]-
Note: Date of deposit in colophon of first issue: 1er trimestre
    1976

, [1988]-
Note: Page [4] of cover of first issue: c1988
```

4D5.3. If the date of copyright or deposit does not represent the probable date of publication, distribution, etc., note it nonetheless and supply a more accurate date of publication, distribution, etc., in square brackets. Provide an explanation for the supplied date, if possible.

4D5.4. If the serial bears both a date of publication, distribution, etc., and a date of copyright or deposit, the latter information may be given in a note, if considered important.

```
, 1880-
Optional note: "Copyright, 1878"--T.p. verso of first issue
```

4E. Place of manufacture

4E1. General rule

Transcribe names of places associated with printers and other manufacturers as part of this element when appropriate according to the instructions in 4A6.

```
Edinburgh : Alexander Strahan and Co. ; London : Sampson Low,
    Son, and Co., 1860-1906 (Edinburgh : Thomas Constable, printer
    to the Queen, and to the University)
```

4E2. Supplied place of manufacture

If the place of manufacture does not appear, or is transcribed as part of another area or element, supply the place of manufacture in square brackets. Use a modern English form of the name, if there is one, and include the name of the larger jurisdiction if considered necessary for identification. Provide a justification for the supplied place in a note if necessary.

```
Boston : Published by J.M. Whittemore, 114 Washington Street
    ([Boston] : Press of Coolidge and Wiley, No. 12 Water Street)
```

4F. Name of manufacturer

Transcribe the names of printers and other manufacturers as part of this element when appropriate according to the instructions in 4A6.

```
Boston : [s.n., 1842-1873] (Boston : Tuttle & Dennett)

Kiel : Bey dem Herausgeber, und Dessau in der Buchhandlung der
    Gelehrten, [1782-1789] (Altona : Gedruckt bey I.D.A. Eckhardt)
```

4G. Date of manufacture

Transcribe a date of impression or other manufacture as part of this element only if it has not been treated as the date of publication, distribution, etc., following the instructions in 4A6.

5. PHYSICAL DESCRIPTION AREA

Contents:
5A.   Preliminary rule
5B.   Extent
5C.   Illustration
5D.   Size and format
5E.   Accompanying material

5A. Preliminary rule

5A1. Prescribed punctuation

For instructions on the use of spaces before and after prescribed punctuation, see 0E.

Precede this area by a period-space-dash-space *or* start a new paragraph.

Precede an illustration statement by a colon.

Precede the size by a semicolon.

Enclose a statement of format in parentheses.

Precede a statement of accompanying material by a plus sign.

Enclose physical details of accompanying material in parentheses.

5A2. Sources of information

Take information for this area from the serial itself.

5B. Extent

5B1. General rule

5B1.1. If the complete extent of the serial is known, record the number of bibliographic units in arabic numerals followed by the specific material designation, which is "v." for printed serials.

```
Bibliographic units: Vol. 1, no. 1-vol. 6, no. 12
Physical units: 72
Record extent as: 6 v.
```

5B1.2. If a serial has continuous numbering with only one level of enumeration, record the number of issues.

```
Bibliographic units: Numb. 1 (Apr. 12, 1709)-numb. 271 (Dec. 30,
   1710)
Physical units: 271
Record extent as: 271 v.
```

5B1.3. If the serial is still being published, or if the extent is unknown, record only the specific material designation "v."

5B2. Reissued serials

For reissued serials, record the number of physical volumes.

```
Bibliographic units: Vol. 1-vol. 2
Physical units: 2
Note: Individual issues have designations: v. 1: No. 1 (April 12,
   1709)-no. 151 (July 1, 1710); v. 2: No. 152 (July 3, 1710)-no.
   271 (Jan. 2, 1711)
Note: Reissue. Originally published weekly: London: J. Morphew,
   1709-1711
Record extent as: 2 v.
```

5B3. Continuously paged serials

If the serial is continuously paged, record the number of physical volumes in the extent area. *Optionally,* give the pagination in parentheses after the number of volumes.

```
4 v. (xii, 364 p.)
```

5C. Illustration

5C1. General rule

5C1.1. To indicate the presence of illustration, use the abbreviation "ill." after the statement of extent.

```
8 v. : ill.
```

5C1.2. *Optionally,* disregard minor illustrations.

5C1.3. Do not regard ornaments (e.g., head-pieces, vignettes, tail-pieces, printers' devices), pictorial covers, or pictorial dust jackets as illustrations. If considered important, these may be mentioned in a note.

5C1.4. *Optionally*, treat significant title-page illustrations as illustrations rather than ornaments. Make a note to indicate any title-page illustration so treated, if considered important.

5C1.5. *Optionally*, add the graphic process or technique in parentheses, preferably using a term found in a standard thesaurus.[16] Give more detailed descriptions of the illustrations in a note, if considered important.

```
: ill. (woodcuts)

: ill. (steel engravings)

: ill. (collotypes)
```

5C2. Types of illustrations

5C2.1. *Optionally*, specify particular types of illustrations. Use in alphabetical order one or more such terms as the following: coats of arms, diagrams, facsims., forms, geneal. tables, maps, music, plans, ports. (use for single or group portraits), samples.

5C2.2. Replace "ill." with terms specifying particular types of illustrations if the particular types are the only illustrations in the serial.

```
: maps

: ports. (Woodburytypes)
```

5C2.3. Precede terms specifying particular types of illustrations with "ill." if the particular types are not the only illustrations in the serial.

```
: ill., maps, plans

: ill. (wood engravings), maps (lithographs)
```

---

[16] Thesauri useful for this purpose include Art & Architecture Thesaurus Online and Thesaurus for Graphic Materials.

5C3. Color illustrations

5C3.1. Describe color illustrations as such using the abbreviation "col." Treat illustrations printed with a tint block (e.g., chiaroscuro woodcuts, tinted lithographs) as color illustrations.

```
: col. ill.

: ill., col. maps, ports. (some col.)

: ill. (some col.), maps, plans

: col. ill. (Baxter prints)
```

5C3.2. Do not describe hand-colored illustrations as "col." unless there is evidence that the serial was issued with the hand coloring. In case of doubt, consider any machine-press serial with hand coloring to have been issued that way by the publisher. Always mention publisher-issued hand coloring in a note (see 7B12); make a local note on the presence of other hand coloring, if considered important (see 7B22).

```
: ill. (some col.)
Note: A weekly horticultural magazine known for its hand colored
    plates of fruits and flowers; see American periodicals series
    online, 1740-1900
```

5C3.3. If both the text and illustrations are printed in a single color, do not describe the illustrations as "col." Make a note to indicate the color of the ink, if considered important.

```
: ill.
Optional note: Printed in green throughout
```

5C4. Serials consisting entirely or chiefly of illustrations

If a serial consists entirely or chiefly of illustrations, account for this fact by specifying "all ill." or "chiefly ill." *Optionally*, when the illustrations are all or chiefly of a particular type (see 5C2.2), replace "ill." with the term specifying the particular type.

```
: all ill.

: chiefly maps
```

5D. Size and format

5D1. General rule

5D1.1. Give the height of a serial (based on the volume(s) or issue(s) in hand) in centimeters, rounding a fraction of a centimeter up to the next full centimeter. If a serial measures less than 10 centimeters, give the height in millimeters.

> ; 18 cm
>> (*Comment:* A serial measuring 17.1 centimeters in height)

> ; 99 mm
>> (*Comment:* A serial measuring between 98 and 99 millimeters in height)

5D1.2. If a serial is bound, measure the height of the binding. When the height of the serial differs by 3 centimeters or more from the height of the binding, specify both.

> ; 12 cm bound to 20 cm

5D1.3. For hand-press serials, add the bibliographical format of the serial in parentheses following the size statement whenever the format can be determined. *Optionally*, give the format also for machine-press serials. Give the format in abbreviated form (fol., 4to, 8vo, 12mo, etc.). Use "full-sheet" for serials made up of unfolded sheets.

> ; 20 cm (4to)
>> (*Comment:* A serial in quarto)

> ; 20 cm (4to and 8vo)
>> (*Comment:* A serial consisting of a mixture of quarto and octavo sheets)

5D2. Width

If the width of a volume or issue is greater than the height, or less than half the height, give the height x width.

> ; 20 x 32 cm

> ; 20 x 8 cm

5D3. Differing sizes

If the volumes or issues differ in size, give the smallest or smaller size and the largest or larger size, separated by a hyphen.

```
; 24-28 cm
```

5E. Accompanying material

5E1. Accompanying material issued regularly

If a serial and its accompanying material are issued simultaneously (or nearly so) and are intended to be issued together regularly, give the name of the material (using, when appropriate, a specific material designation) at the end of the physical description. Include physical details of the accompanying material, if considered important. If the serial has ceased, give also the number of physical units of accompanying material in arabic numerals, if known.

```
; 24 cm + sound discs

; 58 cm + 296 maps (col. ; 46 x 24 cm or smaller)
```

5E1.2. *Optionally*, describe the accompanying material independently

  or   mention it in a note (see 7B13).

5E2. Accompanying material issued irregularly

If accompanying material is issued irregularly or is issued only once, describe it in a note or ignore it (see 7B13).

6. SERIES AREA

Contents:

6A. Preliminary rule

6A1. Prescribed punctuation

For instructions on the use of spaces before and after prescribed punctuation, see 0E.

Precede this area by a period-space-dash-space.

Enclose each series statement in parentheses.

Precede each parallel title by an equals sign.

Precede other title information by a colon.

Precede the first statement of responsibility by a diagonal slash.

Precede each subsequent statement of responsibility by a semicolon.

Precede the ISSN of a series or subseries by a comma.

Precede the numbering within a series or subseries by a semicolon.

Enclose a date following a numeric and/or alphabetic designation in parentheses.

Precede the title of a subseries, or the designation for a subseries, by a period.

Precede the title of a subseries following a designation for the subseries by a comma.

6A2. Sources of information

6A2.1. The prescribed sources of information for the series area are the series title page, serial title page, cover,[17] caption, masthead, editorial pages, colophon, dust jacket, and rest of the serial, in that order of preference. If the serial has both main series and subseries titles, however, prefer a source containing both titles.

6A2.2. If the series statement, or any of its elements, is taken from a source other than the series title page, make a note to indicate the source.

```
(Cooke's pocket edition of select British classics)
Note: Series statement from serial t.p.
```

6A2.3. If the series statement appears on both the series title page and the serial title page, indicate this in a note, if considered important, and record the text of the latter statement if the two differ.

```
(Archie adventure series)
Optional note: Series statement also appears at head of serial
    t.p.

(Beadle's dime series)
Optional note: Series statement also appears on serial t.p. as
    Dime series
```

6A2.4. If the series statement appears as a stamp or on a label, transcribe it as found and make a note to indicate the presence of the stamp or label.

```
(New poetry series)
Note: Series statement from label on serial t.p.
```

6A2.5. If a series statement is not present in the serial, but reference sources provide evidence that the serial was issued as part of a publisher's series, do not

---

[17] Consider the cover to be a prescribed source only if it was issued by the publisher. Series-like statements present on covers not issued by the publisher usually represent binders' titles and should be treated as copy-specific information. They may be transcribed in a local note, if considered important. In case of doubt, do not consider the cover to be a prescribed source of information.

supply a series statement in the series area. Rather, provide the series information in a note, if considered important.

6A2.6. If the series statement is not present in every issue of the serial, do not transcribe a series statement in the series area. Rather, provide the series information in a note (see 7B14.1).

6A3. Form and order of information

Transcribe series information in the form and order in which it is presented in the source, unless instructed otherwise by specific rules (see 0G).

6B. Title proper of series

6B1. Transcribe the title proper of the series as it appears in the serial, according to the general rules 0B-0G.

```
(Beau fleuve)

(Harrison's British classicks)
```

6B2. If the series title proper includes a statement of responsibility that is grammatically inseparable from other words in the series title proper, transcribe it as part of the series title proper.

```
(Report of the Friends of the Earth)

(Turner & Fisher's new and cheap series)
```

6B3. If the series title includes grammatically inseparable numbering that remains constant with every issue, transcribe it as such.

```
(Bulletin number six of the Bridgewater Society)
```
        (*Comment:* "Number six" appears on each issue)

If the numbering changes from issue to issue, omit this information and replace it with the mark of omission (see 6G1).

```
(Bulletin number ... from Pennsylvania University)
```

6C. Parallel titles of series

6C1. If the source bears a series title in more than one language or script, transcribe as the series title proper the title that is in the language or script of the title proper. If this criterion does not apply, transcribe the title that appears first in the source. Transcribe the remaining title(s), together with any associated information, as parallel series titles. Precede each parallel series title by an equals sign. Make a note to indicate the original position in the source of any transposed titles.

6C2. *Optionally*, if it is considered that the parallel series titles are too numerous to list exhaustively, and that some may be omitted without significant loss of identification, omit parallel series titles after the first, using the mark of omission. Transcribe the omitted title(s), together with any associated information, in a note, if considered important.

6D. Other title information of series

6D1. Transcribe other title information relating to the series, if present, following the series title proper.

6D2. If there are parallel series titles (see 6C), transcribe the other title information after the series title to which it relates. If any parallel titles have been omitted from the transcription, also omit the associated other title information. Transcribe the omitted information in a note, if considered important.

6E. Statements of responsibility relating to series

6E1. Transcribe a statement of responsibility relating to the series, if present, following the series title. If the statement of responsibility does not appear in this position in the source, transpose as needed. Provide details of the transposition in a note. However, if the statement of responsibility is grammatically inseparable from the series title, see 6B2.

```
(Report series / Canadian Wildlife Service)
 Note: "Canadian Wildlife Service" appears within decorative
    border at head of title
```

6E2. Parallel statements of responsibility relating to series

6E2.1. If there are parallel series titles (see 6C) but the statement of responsibility relating to the series appears in only one language or script, transcribe the statement of responsibility after the last parallel title (following any other title information associated with the title).

6E2.2. If the statement of responsibility appears in more than one language or script, transcribe each statement after the series title (or other title information) to which it relates.

6E2.3. If any parallel series titles have been omitted from the transcription, also omit their associated statements of responsibility. Transcribe the omitted statement(s) in a note, if considered important.

6F. ISSN of series

Transcribe an International Standard Serial Number (ISSN) of a series if it appears in the serial.

```
(Life Rattle new writers series, ISSN 1200-5266)
```

6G. Numbering within series

6G1. General rule

6G1.1. If all or part of the series numbering remains constant with every issue, or if the serial consists of only one issue, transcribe the numbering as the last element in the series statement. If the numbering does not appear in this order in the source, transpose it as needed. Provide details of the transposition in a note. However, if the numbering is grammatically inseparable from the series title, see 6B3.

```
(Arno series of contemporary art ; no. 3)
```
(Comment: Issues reprinted in a single volume with a single series statement)

6G1.2. Transcribe the numbering as it appears in the serial. Do not use any abbreviations not present in the source and do not convert roman or spelled-out numerals to arabic.

6G1.3. If series numbering appears without a series title, transcribe the numbering in a note. Provide any additional information about the series (e.g., as found in reference sources) in a note, if considered important.

```
Note: Issues for 1910- have numbering on cover: Volume 7-
```

In case of doubt as to whether a number appearing in the serial is series numbering, transcribe the numbering in a note.

6G2. Change in series numbering

If the series numbering changes with each issue, generally omit numbering; transcribe only the designation (if any) and replace the numeral by the mark of omission.

```
(Cahiers de sémiotique textuelle, ISSN 0766-4124 ; ...)
```

6G3. Numbering relating to parallel series titles

6G3.1. If there are parallel series titles (see 6C) with the same numbering on all volumes or issues of the serial that appear in more than one language or script, transcribe each number after the series title to which it relates (following any other title information or any statement of responsibility associated with the title).

```
(Profiles ; number 6 = Profils ; numéro 6)
```

6G3.2. If the series numbering appears only once, and is consistent on all volumes or issues of the serial, transcribe it after the parallel series title to which it relates. However, if the numbering relates to all, more than one, or none of the parallel series titles, transcribe it at the end of the series statement.

```
(Boletin = Bulletin ; 4)
```

6G3.3. If any parallel series titles have been omitted from the transcription, also omit their associated numbers. Transcribe the omitted number(s) in a note, if considered important.

6H. Subseries

6H1. If both a main series and a subseries appear in the serial, give the details of the main series first, followed by the details of the subseries. If the main series and subseries do not appear in this position in the source, transpose them as needed and provide details of the transposition in a note.

```
(Spalding sports library. Spalding soccer series)

(Ars musices iuxta consignationes variorum scriptorum. Période
   romantique et moderne. Domaine français)
```

6H2. If a phrase such as "new series," "second series," etc., appears with an unnumbered series, transcribe the phrase as a subseries title.

```
(Bulletin. New series)
```

If the phrase appears with a numbered series, consider it to be part of the numbering and transcribe it as such, omitting the numbering and using the mark of omission.

```
(Transactions of the American Philosophical Society ; new ser.,
   vol. ...)

(University publications ; new series, # ...)
```

6H3. If there are parallel series titles (see 6C), transcribe each subseries after the series title to which it relates. If any parallel titles have been omitted from the transcription, also omit their associated subseries. Transcribe the omitted subseries in a note, if considered important.

6J. More than one series statement

The information relating to a single series, or series and subseries, constitutes one series statement. If two or more series statements appear in a serial, transcribe each statement separately.

7. NOTE AREA

Contents:
7A.   Preliminary rule
7B.   Notes

7A. Preliminary rule

7A1. General instructions

7A1.1. Notes qualify and amplify the formal description, especially when the rules for such description do not allow certain information to be included in the other areas. Notes can therefore deal with any aspect of the serial.

7A1.2. Notes, by their nature, cannot be enumerated exhaustively, but can be categorized in terms of the areas of description to which they pertain. In addition to notes relating to these areas, there are notes that do not correspond to any area of the formalized areas of description. Occasionally it may be useful to group together notes that refer to more than one area, for instance when they are all based on one source within the work, such as a privilege statement.

7A1.3. If the description in the areas preceding the note area does not clearly identify the resource being cataloged, make whatever notes are necessary for unambiguous identification. When appropriate, refer to detailed descriptions in standard catalogs or bibliographies. Provide sufficient information to identify the specific source, whether using a general note, a formal "References" note giving the source in prescribed form (see 7B17), or some combination of the two.

7A1.4. Notes may also be made to justify added entries intended for special files of personal or corporate names, titles, genres/forms, physical characteristics, provenance, etc. Whenever possible, use terms taken from lists of controlled vocabularies when making such notes and added entries. Prefer the terminology used in controlled vocabularies lists issued by the RBMS Bibliographic Standards Committee. Terms from other authorized thesauri (e.g., Art & Architecture Thesaurus Online) may also be used as appropriate.

7A1.5. In general, notes are not required, but some notes are required in particular situations and are so indicated in previous rules (e.g., 1E3, 2A2, 4A4) and in some of the rules for this area.[18]

7A2. Punctuation

Start a new paragraph for each note. End each paragraph with a period or other mark of final punctuation.

Separate introductory wording from the main content of a note by a colon followed but not preceded by a space.

7A3. Sources of information

Take information recorded in notes from any suitable source. Square brackets are required only for interpolations within quoted material.

7A4. Form of notes

7A4.1. Order of information. If information in a note corresponds to information found in the title and statement of responsibility, edition, numbering, publication, distribution, etc., physical description, or series areas, usually give the elements of information in the order in which they appear in those areas. In such cases, use prescribed punctuation, except substitute a period for a period-space-dash-space.

```
Publishers vary: Oliver Nelson, at Milton's Head in Skinner Row,
    21 Sept. 1745- ; Alex. M'Culloh, in Skinner-Row, <Feb. 1752->
```

7A4.2. Quotations. Record quotations from the serial or from other sources in quotation marks. Follow the quotation by an indication of its source, unless that source is the title page. Do not use prescribed punctuation within quotations.

```
Publication ceased 28 March 1642, "the House of Commons having
    resolved that all unlicensed newspapers should be suppressed"--
    Frank, J.  The beginnings of the English newspaper

"Extracted from the minutes of the Society for the Propagation of
    the Gospel in Foreign Parts"
```

---

[18] A complete list of required notes may be found in the Index under "Required notes."

```
"Generally considered to be by William Langland"--Harvey, P.
   Oxford companion to Engl. lit.
```

7A4.3. Formal notes. Use formal notes employing an invariable introductory word or phrase or a standard verbal formula when uniformity of presentation assists in the recognition of the type of information being presented or when their use provides economy of space without loss of clarity.

7A4.4. Informal notes. When making informal notes, use statements that present the information as briefly as clarity, understandability, and good grammar permit.

7A5. Notes citing other editions and works

7A5.1. Other editions. In citing another edition of the same work, give enough information to identify the edition cited.

```
Other edition: Medical and philosophical commentaries.
   Philadelphia, Penna. : T. Dobson, 1793-1797
```
(Comment: Title of edition being cataloged: Medical commentaries. -- Edinburgh : Anderson, 1783)

7A5.2. Other works and other manifestations of the same work. In citing other works and other manifestations of the same work (other than different editions with the same title), give whatever information is appropriate, such as the main entry heading, title proper (or uniform title), statement of responsibility, edition statement, or date of publication. Arrange the information provided in the form that makes most sense in the particular case. Abridge the information as needed without using the mark of omission.

```
Other edition: California weekly courier (San Francisco, Calif. :
   Steamer)
```

7B. Notes

Some of the most common types of notes are listed below; other notes than those provided for may be made, if considered important. Specific applications of many of these notes are provided in the preceding sections. Make notes as called for in the following subrules, and, generally, in the order in which they are listed here. If a particular note is of primary importance, it may be given first, regardless of its order in this list. When appropriate, combine two or more notes to make one note.

7B1. Frequency

7B1.1. Make notes on the frequency of the serial even if the frequency is apparent from the rest of the description. (The examples given here do not constitute an exhaustive list.)

```
Annual

Quarterly

Daily

Daily (except Sunday)

Published every ten days during the months of the French
   Revolutionary calendar
```

7B1.2. Also make notes on changes in frequency. Date(s) or approximate date(s) associated with each frequency are required. Use abbreviations as found in AACR2, Appendix B.

```
Quarterly, 1712
Monthly, 1699-1711

Monthly, <Nov. 1903>-Apr. 1950
Bimonthly, Jan./Feb. 1898-<July/Aug. 1903>
```

7B2. Language and script of serial; translation or adaptation

7B2.1. Make notes on the language and script of the serial, or on the fact that it is a translation or adaptation, unless this is apparent from the rest of the description.

```
Parallel French and English texts

Text in German and Italian

Text includes some printing in Bengali and Devanagari characters
```

7B2.2. Always note the presence of nonroman script in the serial if it has been transcribed only in romanized form in the description (see 0F2.1).

```
Church Slavic in Cyrillic script

Title in Greek script
```

7B3. Source of title proper

Always make a note on the source of the title proper, even if it is the title page. Combine the "Source of title" note with the "Description based on" note (see 7B21.1).

```
Description based on: Number 1 (Saturday, March 27, 1790); title
    from caption

Description based on: Première année, no 1 (1er juin 1889); title
    from title page

Description based on: Issue for 1849; title from caption

Description based on: Volume IV (1863); title from cover

Description based on: Vol. II, numb. 99 (Thursday, October 4,
    1787); title from masthead
```

7B4. Variations in title

7B4.1. Other titles

7B4.1.1. Make notes on titles borne by the serial other than the one chosen as the title proper. If nonroman text has been transcribed in the title proper without parallel romanization (e.g., as transcribed from the source or provided by 0F2.2), give a romanization of the title proper.

```
Wrapper title: The macaroni and theatrical magazine, or, Monthly
    register ...

Wrapper title: Numb. ... of The gentleman's museum, for ...

Distinctive title: No. 1: Remarks upon the tragedy of Venice
    preserv'd

Running title: Parliamentary debates

Caption title: Historical and political mercury

Individual issues for Mar. 3-June 30, 1821 have caption title:
    Gossip

Romanized title: Zhurnal geofiziki i meteorologii
Note: Romanization supplied by cataloger

Title page reads: BLM Bonniers litterära magasin
```
        (*Comment:* Title proper: Bonniers litterära magasin)

7B4.1.2. If considered important, also include partial or complete transcriptions of title information to show the actual wording of the title page (e.g., when information has been omitted or elements have been transposed), explanations of cataloger-supplied letters or words (e.g., when special marks of contraction have been used by the printer in continuance of the manuscript tradition), and values of punctuation substituting for letters.

```
Marks of contraction and abbreviation in title have been expanded

The r---l register is The royal register
```

7B4.1.3. Make notes on titles by which the serial is commonly known, if considered important.

```
Commonly referred to as: Martin's magazine
```
      (*Comment:* Title appears as: The general magazine of arts and sciences, philosophical, philological, mathematical, and mechanical / by Benjamin Martin)

```
Also known as: Bagwell papers
```
      (*Comment:* Title appears as: The occasional paper)

7B4.1.4. If the title proper on the volume or issue used as the basis of the description has a typographical error(s) make a note on the corrected title, if considered important.

```
Corrected title: The post-man and the historical account
```
      (*Comment:* Title appears as: The post-man and the historical accunt)

7B4.1.5. If the title proper on any volume or issue (other than the volume or issue used as the basis of the description) has a typographical error(s) make a note, if considered important.

```
No. 3 has title: The post-man and the historical accunt
```

7B4.1.6. Record a binder's title in a local note, if considered important. This does not refer to spine titles that appear on publisher-issued bindings common to all copies of an edition or issue (see 7B22.3).

7B4.1.7. If individual issues of a serial (other than a monographic series) have special titles, make a note on the individual titles if considered important.

```
No. 2 also has title: Pressed curtains
```
      (*Comment:* Title is: Curtains)

7B4.2. At head of title. Occasionally a phrase or name that is clearly neither part of the title nor a statement of responsibility appears at the head of the title. Use an "At head of title" note for these and any other indeterminate cases.

```
At head of title: Number I. To be continued weekly

At head of title: Dedicated to the British Senate
```

7B4.3. Minor change in title proper. Make notes on minor changes in the title proper that occur after the first/earliest volume or issue (see 1B7). If scattered volumes or issues have a different title proper, a general statement may be made. Make notes on fluctuating titles. Include corresponding numbering, if appropriate.

```
Title varies slightly

Title appears variously as: Clown war, Clwn wr, Cloud war, Cl'wn
   w'r

Title fluctuates between: New-York legal observer, v. 1, no. 1
   (Oct. 1, 1842)-v. 3, no. 6 (May 15, 1844); New York legal
   observer, v. 3 (Mar. 1, 1845)-v. 4 (Dec. 1846); New-York legal
   observer, v. 5 (Jan. 1847)-v. 11 (Dec. 1853); New York legal
   observer, v. 12 (Jan.-Nov./Dec. 1854)

Title fluctuates between: Chillicothe semi-weekly constitution;
   and: Chillicothe weekly constitution, <Dec. 12, 1898>-Feb. 23,
   1899
```

7B5. Parallel titles and other title information

7B5.1. Make notes on parallel titles appearing in the serial but not on the title page; also give other title information appearing in the serial but not on the title page if it is considered important. If parallel titles and other title information appearing on the title page have been omitted from the title and statement of responsibility area (e.g., because they could not be fitted into the body of the entry, or because they were very lengthy), they may be given here as notes.

7B5.2. Change in parallel title or other title information. Make notes on changes in parallel titles or other title information that occur after the first/earliest volume or issue, if considered important. If the changes have been numerous, a general statement may be made.

```
Subtitle varies; with no. 230 (Feb. 1973) subtitle dropped
   altogether
```

```
French title dropped <Mar./June 1995- >

Parallel title varies
```

7B6. Statements of responsibility

7B6.1. Statement of responsibility not transcribed. Make notes on statements of responsibility that are not transcribed in the title and statement of responsibility area, if considered important.

```
Official journal of: Oklahoma Live Stock Association

Editor: Oliver Goldsmith

No. 1- signed at end: Richard Carlile
```

7B6.2. Fuller form of name. Give a fuller form of the name of a person or corporate body that is transcribed only in abbreviated form elsewhere in the description, if considered important.

```
Full name of Institute: Young Men's Institute
```

7B6.3. Transposed statements of responsibility. Note the original position on the title page of statements of responsibility that have been transposed to the title and statement of responsibility area (see also 7B4.2).

```
On t.p., editor's name precedes title
```

7B6.4. Attributions

7B6.4.1. If a statement of responsibility for a person or corporate body connected with the work does not appear in the serial, and an attribution is available, give the information in a note. Include the authority for the attribution whenever possible.

```
Editor and contributor: Oliver Goldsmith

Edited by Samuel Parker and George Ridpath; see Nelson & Seccombe
```

7B6.4.2. If a statement of responsibility recorded in the title and statement of responsibility area or in a note is known to be fictitious or incorrect, make a note stating the true or most generally accepted attribution. Give the authority for the information whenever possible.

```
Caleb d'Anvers is a pseudonym for the editor, Nicholas Amherst,
    and other chief contributors including Henry, Viscount
    Bolingbroke, and William Pulteney, Earl of Bath; see DNB
```
> (*Comment:* Title page reads: The country journal, or, The craftsman / by Caleb D'Anvers, of Gray's-Inn, Esq.)

7B6.4.3. False attributions appearing in the bibliographical literature or in library catalogs may also be noted, along with the authority for the false attribution and the authority for questioning it.

```
Attributed to Mr. Smith (see Morgan, W.T.  Bibliography of
    British history (1700-1715), V26) and to Wm. Smith the
    antiquary (see Graham, W.  English literary periodicals;
    although DNB does not associate The British Apollo with him);
    dedication of later eds. signed by Marshal Smith
```

7B6.5. Other statements. Record the names of persons or bodies connected with a work, or with previous editions of it, if they have not already been named in the description; give the authority for the information, if necessary.

```
At head of title from no. <67>-1012: Francis Dickson
```

```
Edited and written by "John Gifford," i.e. John Richards Green;
    one of the most important contributing editors was Andrew
    Bisset; another important contributor was John Whitaker; see
    NCBEL
```

7B6.6. Variant forms of names. Note variant forms of names of persons or bodies named in statements of responsibility if the variant forms clarify the names used in main or added entry headings.

```
Edward Ward is the author of A trip to Jamaica
```
> (*Comment:* Statement of responsibility reads: "by the author of The trip to Jamaica")

7B6.7. Change in statements of responsibility. Make notes on changes in statements of responsibility that occur after the first/earliest volume or issue, if considered important (see 1E15). If the changes have been numerous, a general statement may be made.

```
First translator and editor: Henry Rhodes; later editors include
    John Phillips; attributed also to Jean de Fonvive; see Nelson &
    Seccombe
```

```
Editors: 1680-1738, Jean-Alexandre de La Font; 1738-1798, Etienne
    Luzac (with Jean Luzac, 1772-1798); 1798-1811, Abraham Blussé
    (with J.C. Texier Westmuller, 1804-1810?)
```

```
Editor varies
```

7B7. Bibliographic history and relationships with other serials

Make notes on the bibliographic history and on important relationships, if readily known, between the serial being described and the immediately preceding, immediately succeeding, or simultaneously issued serials.

7B7.1. Continuation

7B7.1.1. If a serial continues a previously published serial, make a note citing the preceding serial.

```
Continues: Coq (Paris, France)

Continues: News from abroad, or, The Manchester weekly news
    letter
```

7B7.1.2. If a serial is continued by a subsequently published serial, make a note citing the succeeding serial. *Optionally*, give the date of the change.

```
Continued by: British journal (London, England : 1729)

Continued, in alternate weeks, by: The Bristol oracle, and
    country intelligencer; and: The Bristol oracle and country
    advertiser

Continued by the publishers as: The present state of the
    republick of letters; another continuation, begun by the editor
    in 1730, has title: Literary journal, or, A continuation of the
    Memoirs of literature
```

7B7.2. Merger

7B7.2.1. If a serial is the result of the merger of two or more other serials, make a note citing the serials that were merged.

```
Merger of: Burbage's Nottingham chronicle; and: Creswell's
    Nottingham, Newark, Retford, and Worksop journal
```

7B7.2.2. If a serial is merged with one or more other serials to form a serial with a new title, make a note citing the serial(s) with which it has merged and the new serial.

```
Merged with: Carlisle arrow, to become: Carlisle arrow and red
    man
```

7B7.3. Split

7B7.3.1. If a serial is the result of the split of a previous serial into two or more serials, make a note citing the serial that has been split.

```
Continues in part: Wesleyan Methodist Church in Canada.
   Missionary Society. Nova Scotia and New Brunswick Auxiliary.
   Annual report of the Wesleyan Missionary Auxiliary Society for
   the District of Nova-Scotia, New-Brunswick and Prince Edward
   Island
```

7B7.3.2. If a serial splits into two or more separate serials, make a note citing the serials resulting from the split.

```
Split into: Daily Ipswich journal; and: Weekly Ipswich journal
```

7B7.3.3. If a serial has separated from another serial, make a note citing the serial of which it was once a part.

```
Separated from: Post boy (London, England : 1695 : Roper)
```

7B7.4. Absorption

7B7.4.1. If a serial absorbs another serial, make a note citing the serial absorbed. *Optionally,* give the date of absorption.

```
Absorbed: Glasgow courant
```

```
Absorbed: Everyday housekeeping, Mar. 1912; and: Home needlework
   magazine, May 1917
```

7B7.4.2. If a serial is absorbed by another serial, make a note citing the absorbing serial.

```
Absorbed by: Glasgow journal
```

7B7.5. Translation

7B7.5.1. If a serial is a translation of a previously published serial (as opposed to a different language edition of a serial, for which see 2B1), make a note citing the original (see also 7B7.6).

```
Translation of: Mercure britannique
```

7B7.5.2. If a serial is translated, make a note citing the translation.

```
Translated as: British mercury, or, Historical and critical views
    of the events of the present times
```

7B7.5.3. If unable to cite the original language serial, a general statement may be made.

```
Translation of the German ed.
```

7B7.6. Simultaneous edition

7B7.6.1. If a serial is one of two or more editions differing in partial content and/or in language, make a note citing the other edition(s).

```
Italian ed. of: Mercure britannique
```

```
Issued also in other editions: Field & stream (West ed.); Field &
    stream (South ed.); Field & stream (Midwest ed.); Field &
    stream (Far west ed.)
```

7B7.6.2. If unable to cite the other edition, a general statement may be made.

```
Issued also in French
```

7B7.6.3. If a serial is published in more editions than can be cited conveniently, a general statement may be made.

```
Numerous other editions published
```

7B7.7. Supplement

7B7.7.1. If a serial is a supplement to another serial, make a note citing the main serial.

```
Supplement to: Carpenter's political compendium
```

```
Issued between issues of: Iconograph (New York, N.Y.)
```

7B7.7.2. If a serial has supplement(s) that are described separately, make notes citing the supplement(s).

```
Has supplement: Photography of the year
```

```
Has supplement listing rules, regulation and procedures of the
    Relocation Center: Heart Mountain sentinel bulletin
```

7B7.7.3. Make a brief general statement on irregular, informal, numerous, or unimportant supplements that are not described separately or as accompanying material.

```
Numerous supplements

With occasional supplements, dated and numbered with the regular
    issues

Includes supplements
```

7B7.8. Issued with. For a serial issued with one or more other serials, make a note citing the other serials. Preface this note with the words "Issued with" and a colon.

```
Issued with: Hoard's dairyman
```
> (*Comment:* Each no. of The Jefferson County union issued with an issue of Hoard's dairyman)

```
Issued with: The gentleman's and citizen's almanack ... for the
    year of our Lord ...
```
> (*Comment:* Each no. of The treble almanack for the year ... issued with an issue of The gentleman's and citizen's almanack ...)

7B7.9. Reissue. If a serial is a reissue of another serial, make a note giving details of the original serial, if considered important (see Appendix J).

```
Reissue. Originally published weekly as: The craftsman. London,
    1726-1727

Reissue. Originally published daily (except Sunday), 1711-1712,
    and three times a week, 1714 (publication suspended between no.
    555 (Dec. 6, 1712) and no. 556 (June 18, 1714)): London :
    Printed for Sam. Buckley ... and sold by A. Baldwin ..., [1711-
    1714]; principal contributors: Joseph Addison, Richard Steele
```

7B8. Edition

7B8.1. Note the source of any element of the edition area when it is taken from elsewhere than the title page. Note the original position of any element that is transposed to another position in transcription.

```
The statement "amplified edition" precedes title on t.p.
```

7B8.2. If a statement as to a limited number of copies of the edition appears, give this statement of limitation in a note, if considered important.

```
Each issue published in a limited edition of 150 copies
```

```
Each issue includes a statement of limitation

Vol. 1 limited to 140 copies; v. 2 to 410 copies; v. 3-4 to 300
   copies

"Es gibt 25 Exemplare"--12. Sonderausgabe, colophon
```

7B8.3. If the statement of limitation is accompanied by statements of responsibility or other information relating to the production of the edition, include as much of the additional information in the note as is considered important.

```
"This edition of ... copies is set in 12-point Monotype Caslon
   and printed at The Whittington Press on Sommerville Laid and
   Zerkall Halbmatt papers. The colour plates and half-tones are
   printed at The Senecio Press. The wood-engravings are printed
   from the wood, and the line blocks are made by Keene Engraving.
   ... copies are bound in stiff covers, and ... copies in boards
   covered in Whittington marbled paper, by Smith Settle & Co."--
   Colophon
```

7B8.4. If the statement of limitation includes the unique number of the copy being cataloged, give only the statement of limitation here. Give the copy number in a separate local note, if considered important (see 7B22).

```
No. 4: Limited ed. of 590 copies
Optional local note: No. 4: Bancroft Library has no. ix of 590
   copies
```

7B8.5. Make notes on changes in edition information that occur after the first/earliest volume or issue, if considered important (see 2B9). If the changes have been numerous, a general statement may be made.

```
"American edition" dropped with v. 2
```

7B9. Numbering and issuing peculiarities

7B9.1. Beginning and/or ending numbering not recorded in the numbering area

7B9.1.1. If the beginning and/or ending numbering is not recorded in the numbering area (see 3A1), make notes on beginning and/or ending numbering, if known.

```
Ceased with no. 3

Began with Nov. 12, 1800
```

7B9.1.2. Information may come from the volume(s) or issue(s) in hand, the publisher (distributor, etc.), or reference sources. Give the source of this information at the end of the note.

```
Began with: 20 Dec. 1737. See NCBEL

Ceased with 1840. See Bib. der Schweizerischen Landeskunde
```

7B9.1.3. When neither the first nor last volume or issue is in hand, give a single note for both the beginning and ending numbering, if known.

```
Began in 1731? Ceased in 1741. See NCBEL
```

7B9.2. Complex or irregular numbering. Make notes on complex or irregular numbering of a serial not already specified in the numbering area, if considered important. Make notes on issuing peculiarities, if considered important.

```
Numbering irregular

Nov. 21, 1888 issue misdated Nov. 12, 1888

Issues for Nov. 1-6 have continuous pagination and are called v.
   1

Errors in numbering with many numbers repeated

Gregorian calendar designation added with issue for Feb. 26,
   1803; French Republican calendar designation dropped with issue
   for Jan. 4, 1806; numbering irregular
```

7B9.3. Period covered. If the period covered by a volume or issue of a serial issued annually or less frequently is other than a calendar year, make a note on the period covered.

```
Report year ends Sept. 30

Each issue covers: Apr. 1-Mar. 31

Annual compilation based on the racing season, usually Apr. to
   Nov.
```

7B9.4. Pilot or introductory issues. If a pilot or sample issue precedes the first issue of the serial, make a note, if considered important.

```
Number 1 preceded by a number dated Oct. 1967 called 0

Preceded by a "Prospecto," 21 de mayo de 1821
```

```
Preceded by a volume called "almost first edition" in 1991
```
   (*Comment:* First edition was 1993)

7B10. Publication

7B10.1. Make notes on publication details that are not included in the publication, distribution, etc., area if they are considered important. If elements of the publication, distribution, etc., area have been taken from a source outside the serial itself, make a note specifying the source.

```
Imprint from colophon, no. 3

Publication date from Evans
```

7B10.2. If a serial suspends publication with the intention of resuming at a later date, make a note. If publication is resumed give the dates or designation of the period of suspension.

```
Suspended Aug. 17-Sept. 23, 1845
```

7B10.3. Make notes on any significant variations, peculiarities, irregularities, etc., concerning the serial's publication, printing, distribution, etc.

```
Imprints lack dates; years of publication from dates of issues

Imprint from colophon; imprint lacks date

Publisher's statement appears in note at end of text: "Published
   by S. Bagster, 81 Strand; sold by the booksellers and the
   newsmen, price 4d"

Place of publication assumed by cataloger
```

7B10.4. Change in publication, distribution, etc. Make a note on changes in place and/or publisher, distributor, etc., appearing on later volumes or issues.

```
Place of publication varies: Issue 2-  Bisbee, Arizona

Vols. for 1877- published: Muskogee, I.T. : Indian Journal Steam
   Job Print
```

7B11. Signatures

Make a note giving details of the signatures of a serial, if considered important. Give these signature details generally according to DCRM(B) 7B9. Preface this note with the word "Signatures" and a colon.

Signatures: v. 1: pi^2 A-2B^8 2C^2; v. 2: pi^2 A-2B^8; v. 3: pi^2 A-2B^8;
   v. 4: pi^2 A-2B^8; v. 5: pi^2 A-2A^8; v. 6: pi^2 A-2A^8; v. 7: pi^2 A-V^8;
   v. 8: pi^2 A-2F^8 [2G]^2

Signatures: [A]^4 B-C^4 D^2 E-G^4 H^2
   (*Comment:* A serial reissued in one volume)

Omit signature statements if there are too many volumes, or if the collation is too complex.

7B12. Physical description

7B12.1. Make notes on important physical details that are not already included in the physical description area, if considered important. Describe a modern publisher-issued binding, if considered important.

    Bound in yellow cloth with bamboo design in gold, red and green

7B12.2. Give the number of columns if more than one, if considered important.

    Printed in 2 columns

7B12.3. If other physical details are deleted or changed in a subsequent volume or issue, make notes if considered important.

7B13. Accompanying material

Make notes for any accompanying material not recorded in the physical description area. Give the location of accompanying material if appropriate.

    Each issue accompanied by an original drawing

    No. 1 accompanied by: "Star guide" (1 sheet ; 12 x 36 cm),
       previously published separately in 1744

7B14. Series

7B14.1. Note the source of any element of the series area when it is taken from elsewhere than the series title page. If any element has been transposed in the description, note its original position in the serial. Make a note on series information that does not appear on all issues of a serial. Note any other series information not transcribed in the series area, if considered important. Give information about a series in which the serial has been issued previously, if considered important.

```
Series numbering precedes series title

Series statement from serial t.p.

Vol. 1-4 have series statement "Parson's select British classics"
   and are numbered no. 18-21
```

7B14.2. Make a note on the numbering within a series if the numbering varies from issue to issue, if considered important.

7B14.3. Make notes about minor changes in series statements that occur after the first/earliest volume or issue, if considered important.

7B15. Other formats

Make a note of other formats in which the content or partial content of the serial is, or has been, issued.

```
Also issued on microfilm

Vols. 100-103 also issued on microcards
```

7B16. Indexes

Make notes on the presence of cumulative indexes. If possible, give the type of index, the volumes, etc., of the serial indexed, the dates of the serial indexed, and the location of the index in the set, or the numbering of the index if it is issued separately. Make a note also on separately published indexes.

```
Indexes: Vols. 1 (1827)-5 (1831) in v. 6, no. 1

Index published separately every Dec.
```

7B17. References to published descriptions

7B17.1. Give references to published descriptions in bibliographies or other authoritative reference sources if these have been used to supply elements of the description. Use the form and punctuation conventions recommended by *Standard Citation Forms for Published Bibliographies and Catalogs Used in Rare Book Cataloging*. Begin the note with the word "References" and a colon.

7B17.2. Make other references to published descriptions, if considered important. Such references are especially useful whenever the cited source would serve to distinguish an edition (or variant) from similar editions (or variants), substantiate information provided by the cataloger, or provide a more detailed description of the serial being cataloged.

```
References: Nelson & Seccombe, 355

References: NCBEL, II, col. 1288

References: Hoffman, F.J.  Little magazine, 388

References: ESTC T177671

References: Times handlist, p. 46

References: Barth, H.  Bib. der Schweizer Geschichte, 32226
```

7B17.3. A general note may be made if a description of the serial being cataloged does not appear in a specific bibliographical reference source. Make such a note only if the serial fits the scope for that source and the source purports to be comprehensive for its scope. Preface the general note with the words "Not in" and a colon.

```
Not in: Nelson & Seccombe
```

7B18. Summary

Give a brief summary of the content of the serial, if considered important.

```
Includes ephemerides, charts of planetary positions on specific
    dates, essays on dreams, prophecies, magic and alchemy,
    biographies of magicians, puzzles and magic tricks for readers,
    and current news featuring psychic and paranormal events

Polemic and satiric attacks on the Test Act and its effects upon
    morals, politics, and religion
```

7B19. Contents

7B19.1. Make notes on inserts, other serials included in the serial, and important special items with specific titles. Do not give contents notes for monographic series.

```
Issues for 1789-1792 include numbered articles: The theatrical
    observer, no. 1-45
```

7B19.2. Transcribe contents from the title page if they are presented there formally, remain the same from issue to issue, and are grammatically separable from the title proper and other title information. In such cases, follow the word "Contents" with a colon and the parenthetical phrase "(from t.p.)."

```
Contents: (from t.p.) I. John Watson Stewart's almanack -- II.
    Exshaw's English court registry -- III. Wilson's Dublin
    directory with a new correct plan of the city, forming the most
    complete lists published of the present civil, military and
    naval establishments of Great Britain & Ireland
```

7B20. Numbers

Make notes of any numbers associated with the serial not transcribed in another area, if considered important.

7B21. Basis of the description

7B21.1. Always make a note of the volume or issue upon which the description is based. Combine the "Description based on" note with the "Source of title" note (see 7B3). Give the numbering for the volume or issue cited in the same order as in the numbering area, and with the appropriate prescribed punctuation.

```
Description based on: Num. 1 (December 29, 1668); title from
    caption

Description based on: Tom. I (ad annum MDCCXLVII et MDCCLXVIII);
    title from cover

Description based on: Volume I, number 1 (June 10, 1867); title
    from title page

Description based on: Semestre I, num. 1 (del sabado 13 de mayo
    de 1826); title from caption

Description based on: Der erste Theil; title from title page

Description based on: Vol. I, no. 3 (April 1863); title from
    title page

Description based on: No. XVII (11 Sept. 1722); title from
    caption

Description based on: 1e jaargang, no. 11 (18 t/m 24 febr. '44);
    title from caption

Description based on: Numb. II (for the month of September,
    1719); title from caption

Description based on: Vol. I, num. 2 (Wednesday morning,
    September 10, 1800); title from masthead
```

Descriptive Cataloging of Rare Materials (Serials)

```
Description based on: Numb. 3 (from Tuesday, the 5. of Sept. to
    Tuesday, the 12. of Sept. 1643) digital surrogate (in EEBO);
    title from caption
```

7B21.2. Always make a note of the latest volume or issue consulted in making the description. Use the appropriate terminology for the type of serial being described (e.g., use "volume" for serials that have volume title pages; use "issue" for serials that do not have volume title pages). Give the numbering for the volume or issue cited in the same order as in the numbering area, and with the appropriate prescribed punctuation.

```
Latest issue consulted: Vol. 1, no. 7 (Thursday, February 19,
    1829)

Latest issue consulted: Part 2, nu. 55 (Tuesday, May 21 to
    Tuesday, May 28 1650)

Latest issue consulted: Numb. 16 (4th to 11th of Apr. 1651)

Latest issue consulted: The sixth part

Latest issue consulted: Numb. IX (Tuesday, March 14, 1738)

Latest issue consulted: No 4 (1re décade de brumaire, an VIII
    [22-31 Oct. 1799])

Latest issue consulted: Boletín no 144 (31 de diciembre de 1967)

Latest volume consulted: Tom. VI (année 1792 a 1800)

Latest volume consulted: 1811/1812

Latest volume consulted: Volume the thirteenth

Latest volume consulted: Anno MDCCLXXIX, pars posterior

Latest volume consulted: Der LXVII. und LXIIX. Theil

Latest volume consulted: Tome trente-neuvième (depuis l'année
    MDCCLXX, jusques & compris l'année MDCCLXXII)
```

7B21.3. The "Description based on" note may not be combined with the "Latest issue consulted" note. Always give the "Latest issue consulted" note as a separate note.

```
Description based on: No. 100 (Saturday, November 29, 1729);
    title from caption
Latest issue consulted: No. 151 (Saturday, November 21, 1730)
```

```
Description based on: Tome premier (comprenant les mois de mars,
   avril & mai 1764); title from title page
Latest volume consulted: Tome huitieme (comprenant les mois de
   décembre 1765, janvier & février 1766)

Description based on: 1855; title from title page
Latest volume consulted: 1870

Description based on: Numb. 1 (Saturday, January 8, 1731/2 [i.e.
   1732]); title from caption
Latest issue consulted: Numb. 86 (from Saturday, September 1 to
   Saturday, September 8, 1733)

Description based on: 1ste jaargang, no. 33 (donderdag, 30
   novembr [sic] 1944); title from caption
Latest issue consulted: 1ste jaargang, no. 104 (zondag, 11
   februari 1945)

Description based on: Vol. 1, no. 10 (Aug. 14, 1798); title from
   caption
Latest issue consulted: Vol. 1, no. 21 (Oct. 30, 1798)

Description based on: Année MDCCLXX; title from title page
Latest volume consulted: Année MDCCLXXIV

Description based on: #1; title from caption
Latest issue consulted: #1
```
   (*Comment:* Only one issue published)

```
Description based on: Numb. 2 (from Thursday, August 1 to
   Thursday, August 8, 1650); title from masthead
Latest issue consulted: Numb. 2 (from Thursday, August 1 to
   Thursday, August 8, 1650)
```
   (*Comment:* Only one issue in hand)

7B22. Copy being described and library holdings (Local notes)

7B22.1. General rule

7B22.1.1. Make local notes on any special features or imperfections of the copy being described when they are considered important. Copy-specific information is highly desirable in the context of rare materials cataloging, which puts greater emphasis on materials as artifacts than is usual in general cataloging practice. Local notes can also provide warrant for added entries (e.g., added entries for the names of former owners or binders, for various kinds of provenance evidence, binding characteristics). Carefully distinguish local notes from other kinds of notes that record information valid for all copies of the bibliographic unit being cataloged.

For many older serials, however, it will not be readily ascertainable whether the characteristics of a single copy are in fact shared by other copies. In case of doubt, consider that the characteristics of the copy in hand are not shared by other copies.

7B22.1.2. The extent and depth of detail provided in local notes will be determined by the local policies of the cataloging agency. The rules set forth in this area are intended primarily to provide guidance and examples; the instructions are not to be seen as prescriptive.

7B22.1.3. Features that may be brought out here include known imperfections and anomalies, provenance evidence (such as bookplates, stamps, autographs, and manuscript annotations), the names of persons or institutions associated with specific copies, copy-specific binding details and the names of binders, copy numbers (see 7B8.4), and "Bound with" notes.

7B22.1.4. Include in local notes one or more of the following identifiers, if considered important: a designation of the holding institution (e.g., a library's name, acronym, or code), a designation of the item's physical location (e.g., a shelfmark), or an indication of the item's copy number (if the institution holds more than one copy). Such identifiers are especially recommended if the bibliographic record is to be contributed to a union catalog or other shared database.

```
Beinecke Library copy: Bound with, in chronological order, issues
    of: Gloucester journal; Felix Farley's Bristol journal; and,
    Bristol gazette; marked by volume numbering of the Gloucester
    journal
```

7B22.2. Provenance

Make a local note to describe details of an item's provenance, if considered important. In less detailed descriptions, it is advisable to summarize provenance information, without providing exact transcriptions or descriptions of the evidence. Include the names of former owners or other individuals of interest and approximate dates, whenever possible.

```
Ms. annotations: Ralph Hodgson: 1-5

Beinecke Library copy: From the library of Samuel Beardsley: 1839
```

More detailed descriptions of provenance might include such additional features as: exact transcriptions of autographs, inscriptions, bookplates, stamps, shelfmarks, etc.; location of each in the item; approximate dates when known; descriptions of bookplates using standardized terminology; descriptions of anonymous heraldic bookplates according to heraldic blazon; references to published descriptions of the collections of former owners of the item, particularly if the item is cited in the source, etc.

```
Beinecke Library copy has presentation inscription to Fania Van
    Vechten from Carl Van Vechten: "To beloved Fania with all love,
    Carlo, Feb. 24, 1955, New York": v. 32, no. 14
```

7B22.3. Bindings

7B22.3.1. Use local notes for descriptions of copy-specific bindings, if considered important; for descriptions of publisher-issued bindings common to all copies of an edition or issue, see 7B12.1.

7B22.3.2. Make a local note, if considered important, whenever a serial has been bound with one or more works subsequent to publication. Preface the note with the words "Bound with" followed by a colon. Formulate the remainder of the note according to the instructions in DCRM(B) 7B18.

```
Special Collections copy bound with: Mercurius pragmaticus.
    (London, England : 21 Sept. 1647)
```

7B22.3.3. If it is considered that the works are too numerous to be listed exhaustively, make an informal note such as the following:

```
Copy 1: Bound with Mercurius melancholicus and 23 other titles;
    ms. list "Old newspapers contained in this volume," laid in
```

7B22.3.4. Make a local note to describe other details of a copy-specific binding, if considered important. Less detailed descriptions might include the color and nature of the covering material, a summary of any decoration present (e.g., "gold-tooled," "blind-tooled"), and (if these can be determined) an approximate date and the name of the binder.

```
British Library copy: late 17th-century binding in red goatskin,
    gold-tooled and blind-stamped
```

7B22.3.5. More detailed descriptions of a binding might include such additional features as: nature of the boards (e.g., wood, paper); details of decoration; country or city of production; nature and decoration of spine; presence or former presence of ties, clasps, or other furniture; flaps; description of headbands, page-edge and end-paper decoration; references to published descriptions or reproductions of the binding (or related bindings), etc.

> British Library copy: late 17th-century English binding; red
>   goatskin, gold-tooled, over paper boards; gold-tooled spine
>   with five raised bands; gilt edges; gold roll on edges of
>   boards; marbled endpapers

8. Standard Number and Terms of Availability Area

Contents:

8A. Preliminary rule

8A1. Prescribed punctuation

For instructions on the use of spaces before and after prescribed punctuation, see 0E.

Precede this area by a period-space-dash-space or start a new paragraph.

Precede each repetition of this area by a period-space-dash-space.

Precede a key-title by an equals sign.

Precede terms of availability by a colon.

Enclose a qualification to the standard number or terms of availability in parentheses.

8A2. Sources of information

Take information included in this area from any source. Do not enclose any information in square brackets.

8B. Standard number

Give the International Standard Serial Number (ISSN). Give such numbers with the abbreviation "ISSN" and with the standard hyphenation.

```
ISSN 0046-225X
```

8C. Key-title

Give the key-title, if it is found in the serial or is otherwise readily available, after the International Standard Serial Number (ISSN). Give the key-title even if it is identical to the title proper. If no ISSN is given, do not record the key-title.

```
ISSN 0261-3093 = Matrix
```

8D. Terms of availability

Optionally, if the serial bears a price or other terms of availability, record the information in this area or give it in a note (see 7B10).

8E. Qualification

Optionally, add qualifications (including the type of binding) to the ISSN and/or terms of availability.

```
ISSN 0023-7108 (glossy paper)
```

APPENDIX A. MARC 21 DESCRIPTIVE CONVENTIONS CODE

A1. Introduction

In MARC 21 bibliographic records, a code may be used in field 040, subfield ‡e, to indicate when specific cataloging conventions have been followed *in addition to* the conventions identified in the descriptive cataloging form (Leader/18). This appendix offers guidance in using "dcrms," the code designating DCRM(S), in 040 subfield ‡e.

A2. Full-level DCRM(S)

Apply the code "dcrms" to records for serials cataloged at full level (i.e., the normative application of these rules). The fact that such records follow the full-level provisions of DCRM(S) is indicated by the blank value assigned in the encoding level (Leader/17) and the code "dcrms" in 040 subfield ‡e. However, do not apply the code "dcrms" to records for serials cataloged only to meet the requirements of the CONSER standard record that do not also meet the requirements of DCRM(S).

A3. Collection-level DCRM(S)

Do not apply the code "dcrms" to records for serials cataloged according to the collection-level guidelines found in Appendix B. The fact that such records contain collection-level descriptions is indicated by the value **c** assigned in the bibliographic level (Leader/07). The guidelines in Appendix B suggest factors to consider in constructing collection-level records for rare materials and provide examples useful in a special collections context. However, the conventions conform substantially to those governing standard collection-level descriptions, as presented in *Cataloging Service Bulletin*, no. 78 (Fall 1997).

A4. Minimal-level DCRM(S)

Apply the code "dcrms" to records for serials cataloged according to the minimal-level guidelines found in Appendix D. The fact that such records follow the minimal-level provisions of DCRM(S) is indicated by the value **7** assigned in the encoding level (Leader/17) and the code "dcrms" in 040 subfield ‡e.

A5. Microforms and digital reproductions of serials

Apply the code "dcrms" to records for microforms and digital reproductions of serials if the descriptive portion of the record conforms to DCRM(S) (full or minimal level). If, however, DCRM(S) (full or minimal level) is not used in all aspects but instead in some "hybrid" fashion, do not use the code "dcrms."

A6. Nontextual serials

Do not apply the code "dcrms" to records for nontextual serials (e.g., music serials, map serials, nonprint serials) not encoded as language material (i.e., value **a**) in type of record (Leader/06), even though they may have been cataloged according to an adapted, "DCRM(S)-like" standard.[19]

A7. Individual and special issues of serials

Do not apply the code "dcrms" to records for individual and special issues cataloged separately as monographs according to the provisions of Appendix H; apply instead the code "dcrmb."

A8. "Special collections cataloging"

In this context "special collections cataloging" means fuller use of notes, access points, and other elements that are not specifically called for in AACR2 or its predecessors, but that follow the spirit of DCRM(S) without following its rules completely. Such cataloging is frequently done for 19th-century and later materials housed in special collections. Do not apply the code "dcrms" to records for "special collections cataloging" unless the cataloging follows the descriptive requirements of DCRM(S) completely (full or minimal level).

A9. Earlier codes

If an existing serial record contains an earlier code in 040 subfield ‡e, such as "dcrb" (*Descriptive Cataloging of Rare Books*) and the description is being updated to DCRM(S) standards, delete the earlier code and add the "dcrms" code to the end of the 040 field in subfield ‡e.

---

[19] If one exists, use a DCRM component manual for the format being described.

Descriptive Cataloging of Rare Materials (Serials)

APPENDIX B. COLLECTION-LEVEL RECORDS

B1. Introduction

B1.1. This appendix offers guidance in the creation of bibliographic records for collections of printed items that will receive collection-level treatment based on administrative or curatorial decisions. Several rationales can be cited to justify a decision to use collection-level cataloging:

- It can be a means of highlighting the shared characteristics of a collection of materials by providing a summary-level description, thereby "adding value" to any other forms of intellectual access, such as item-level records, and revealing collection strengths that may not otherwise be obvious.

- It can be a means of providing temporary control of unprocessed collections.

- It can be a cost-effective means of providing bibliographic control for low-priority items. Although this might seem to promise a solution to the problem of an institution's limited means, it should be understood that adequately arranging and processing collections prior to cataloging also takes time. Since there are significant costs associated with under-cataloged materials, this rationale should be used with careful consideration.

B1.2. A collection-level record may serve as the sole method of access for the collection, with contents information provided in notes. Some or all of the collection may also be represented by item-level bibliographic records, which may be created at any level of fullness using cataloging rules such as AACR2 or components of DCRM. Item-level access may also be provided for some or all of the collection through inventories, finding aids, or databases (referred to hereafter as "finding aids"), which may be linked to collection-level records. Providing some form of item-level access to resources represented by a collection-level record offers significant benefits for users and reduces the risk of redundant acquisition of those resources. Decisions about the appropriate type and level of description should be made based on institutional goals, priorities, and resources, as well as the attributes of the collections themselves.

B1.3. The following guidelines are based on those issued by the Library of Congress for collection-level cataloging published in *Cataloging Service Bulletin,* no. 78 (Fall 1997). Examples have been added, drawn from the types of collections likely to be found in rare books and special collections libraries. Catalogers creating collection-level records will also need to consult the appropriate cataloging rules, *MARC 21 Format for Bibliographic Data*, and their local system documentation in order to create useful, descriptive, and complete records using the various fields available to describe collections, as well as to create additional access points. Catalogers wishing to contribute collection-level records as part of the Program for Cooperative Cataloging will need to consult the relevant instructions in *BIBCO Core Record Standards*.

B1.4. These guidelines are *not* intended for description of traditional archival or manuscript collections. Rules for cataloging such collections are addressed in specialized sets of rules such as *Describing Archives: A Content Standard*. However, many of the activities associated with arranging and describing traditional archival or manuscript collections also pertain to collections of printed materials and inform these guidelines.

B2. Selection of materials

B2.1. Collections normally fall into one of three categories:

‣ groups of items that come to a library already well-organized by a previous owner

‣ groups of items that come from a single source, but with minimal or no previous organization

‣ groups of items that are assembled into collections by the library for the purpose of processing and storage, and are therefore termed "intentionally assembled collections" (previously called "artificial collections")

B2.2. All three types of collections tend to be organized around one or more unifying factors, which may include:

‣ personal author

‣ issuing body

‣ genre/form

‣ subject

‣ language or nationality

‣ provenance

‣ time period

B2.3. Types of materials appropriate to consider for collection-level treatment include:

- groups of materials that share one or more of the above factors, and for which access can adequately be provided with a single classification number and/or a collective set of access points

- groups of pamphlets or ephemera in various formats that are judged not to merit item-level cataloging, but that collectively are of research value

B3. Arrangement and description

B3.1. Arrangement and description are terms used to describe various types of processing activities that bring order and control to collections of materials. They commonly involve the physical handling, sorting, and listing of materials, as well as preservation and housing activities. Additional guidance in these matters may be found in Kathleen Roe's *Arranging and Describing Archives and Manuscripts*.

B3.2. Arrangement. Arrangement is the process of sorting individual items into meaningful groups and placing those groups into useful relationships with each other. Materials can be arranged in many logical ways, and the design of the arrangement should be determined by examining the material to consider the types of access most likely to serve the needs of researchers and other potential users. Different collections will require differing levels and methods of arrangement. For these reasons, decisions about arrangement must be made individually for each collection.

B3.2.1. Organized prior to acquisition. For collections that come to the library already well organized, every effort should be made to maintain this order. Maintaining the original order of a collection can reveal significant information about the previous owner's use of the materials and is, for this reason, a basic tenet of archival practice.

B3.2.2. Organized by the library. Collections that come to the library lacking any recognizable order must be examined, sorted, and arranged in some fashion prior to cataloging. Collections consisting of many items are normally divided into hierarchical subgroupings. Customary types of arrangement include:

- by source or provenance
- by genre/form

- by content or topic

- in chronological order

- in alphabetical order (by author, title, etc.)

B3.2.3. Acquired individually. Materials originally acquired as individual items (whether simultaneously or over time) may be grouped in intentionally assembled collections, as noted above. Appropriate library staff, which may include curators and catalogers, must determine which materials will be so combined, how they will be arranged, and at what level of fullness they will be described (e.g., whether the material will receive contents notes and/or author-title analytics, whether it will be classified and shelved with book collections or boxed and treated archivally).

B3.3 Description. Description is the process of recording the information that was gathered during the sorting and arranging stages. For large collections, finding aids typically are compiled to provide a greater level of detail. Finding aids vary widely in format, style, and complexity. They generally consist of two parts. The first is a narrative introduction that includes: biographical sketches or historical contextual information; a content summary highlighting strengths, gaps, weaknesses, and characterizing the collection's extent and depth; and information concerning the collection's administration and use, such as restrictions on access. The second part is a listing of the items or groups of items that comprise the collection. For collections arranged hierarchically, the listings may stop at a collective subgroup level or may extend down to the file or item level.

B4. Elements of the bibliographic record

The rules that guide the bibliographic description and added entry portions of collection-level cataloging are the latest edition of AACR2, supplemented by use of appropriate national rule interpretations. Use the rules in conjunction with these guidelines, which are arranged by MARC 21 field. Fields for which no specific collection-level instructions are required are not included here but may be used as appropriate.

Leader and directory

> **06**: **Type of record**. If the collection contains only printed, microform, and/or electronic language material (e.g., books, broadsides, pamphlets,

serials), code as Language Material, type **a**. If the collection also includes other material types (e.g., cartographic, music, manuscript), code as Mixed Materials, type **p**.

07: **Bibliographic level**. Use the value **c** (collection-level).

Control field: 008

06: **Type of date.** Coding choices are: **i** (inclusive dates of collection), **k** (range of years of bulk of collection), and **m** (multiple dates).

07-10: **Date 1.** Give the earliest date, or single date, from the 260 field.

11-14: **Date 2**. Give the latest or closing date from the 260 field. Enter **9999** in 008/11-14 if the collection is open or not yet complete and use **m** in 008/06.

15: **Country of publication**. If all the items were published in a single country (or state, province, etc.), enter the code for that country. If the items were published in more than one country, enter the code **vp_**.

1XX field: Main entry

The main entry heading is determined by application of the appropriate cataloging rules. Title main entry is appropriate for many collections (see AACR2 rule 21.7). A 1XX name main entry is appropriate when all materials have the same personal author(s) or emanate from a single corporate body (AACR2 rule 21.4), including collections of laws with main entry under jurisdiction (AACR2 rule 21.31B1).

```
110   1    ‡a Austria.

110   1    ‡a California. ‡b Governor.
```

When a collection is known by the name of its collector, enter the record under the heading for that person or body. *Optionally,* follow the heading by the relator term "collector" in subfield ‡e or the relator code "col" in subfield ‡4.[20]

---

[20] For more information, see the guidelines in RBMS Controlled Vocabularies: Relator Terms for Use in Rare Book and Special Collections Cataloging.

```
100  1   ‡a Purland, Theodocius, ‡e collector.
245  10  ‡a [Theodocius Purland collection of materials on
             mesmerism].
```

240 field: Uniform title

Supply a uniform title for the collection if appropriate according to AACR2 chapter 25.

```
110  1   ‡a Austria.
240  10  ‡a Laws, etc. (Royal decrees)

130  0   ‡a Adventurer (London, England : 1752)
```
      (*Comment:* Collection of miscellaneous editions of The adventurer)

245 field: Title statement

Construct a title for the collection and enclose it in square brackets. Devised titles should generally be in the language and script of the cataloging agency and should be both descriptive and distinctive, thereby highlighting the factor(s) that characterize the collection as a whole. Strive for consistency in title construction across collections. Types of data appropriate for inclusion in collective titles include:

- name of collection (for previously-named collections)

- name of creator, creating body, collector, or source (provenance)

- languages

- geographic locations

- genre/form of material

- principal subjects—persons, events, topics, activities, objects, and dates of subject coverage

```
245  10  ‡a [Association of American Railroads collection of
             pamphlets].

245  00  ‡a [Fanzine collection].

245  00  ‡a [Collection of periodicals and other materials on the
             siege of Paris and the Commune of 1871].

245  10  ‡a [Hyman Bradofsky collection of amateur journalism].

245  00  ‡a [Collection of Dutch clandestine periodicals].

245  00  ‡a [Little blue book collection].
```

246 field: Variant form of title

Record variant titles by which a collection may be known if they differ substantially from the 245 title statement and provide a useful access point. If most or all of the items in the collection have the same title information and it is considered important, make an added entry for the title.

```
245  10   ‡a [William J. Griffith collection on Central America].
246  3    ‡a Griffith Guatemala collection
```

260 field: Publication, distribution, etc. (Imprint)

All elements of the imprint may be included in collection-level records if appropriate. Bracket all elements that are used. In most cases, only the date element (subfield ‡c) is appropriate. Use 260 subfields ‡a, ‡b, ‡e, and ‡f only if the same place and/or the same publisher, printer, or bookseller apply to all items in the collection. If the collection is finite, use a single date or inclusive dates in the subfield ‡c, as appropriate.

```
260       ‡c [1869-2000]

260       ‡c [1780-1860, bulk 1795-1840]

260       ‡a [Paris, ‡c 1870-1874]

260       ‡a [Madrid : ‡b El Partido Nacional, ‡c 1835]-
```

300 field: Physical description

Extent. Give the extent of the collection by counting or estimating the number of items it contains. *Optionally*, provide a separate physical description for each format.

```
300       ‡a 17 v.

300       ‡a 25 items

300       ‡a ca. 350 pieces

300       ‡3 Serials: ‡a 4 cartons, 25 boxes, and 2 oversize boxes
          (16 linear ft.)
```

Other physical details. Provide other details of particular significance.

Dimensions. *Optionally,* provide details of the size of the items and/or their containers. A range of sizes may be used if the items or containers are not of uniform size.

```
300        ‡a ... ; ‡c 28 cm.

300        ‡a ... ; ‡c 23-30 cm.

300        ‡a ... ; ‡c 60 x 90 cm or smaller.

300        ‡a 20 pieces ; ‡c in box 12 x 26 x 35 cm.
```

351 field: Organization and arrangement

Describe the way in which materials have been subdivided into smaller units or the order in which particular units have been arranged.

```
351        ‡a Organized in three series: 1. Timetables. 2.
              Promotional literature. 3. Annual reports.

351        ‡a Items are arranged chronologically.
```

4XX fields: Series statement

Do not use. If series titles of items in the collection are significant, trace them in the appropriate 7XX field. A note supporting the tracing may also be provided.

```
500        ‡a Most of the pieces are from the series Parson's
              edition of select British classics.
730    0   ‡a Parson's edition of select British classics.
```

5XX fields: Notes

Inclusion of a variety of notes will help provide collective context to the materials being described. It is particularly important to describe the contents of the collection in a 505 contents note and/or a 520 summary note, as described below. The order of notes presented below is recommended based on archival collection-level cataloging practice.

500 field: General note

Always include as the first note the statement "Collection title devised by cataloger."

506 field: Restrictions on access

When access to a collection or a portion thereof is restricted, explain the nature and extent of the restrictions.

```
506       ‡a Restricted: Original materials are extremely fragile;
          ‡c Researchers must use microfilm.

506       ‡3 All materials except pamphlets are restricted until
          Jan. 1, 2050.
```

545 field: Biographical or historical note

Provide biographical or historical information about the individual or organization referenced in the 1XX or 245 field.

```
545       ‡a Screenwriter for film and television, playwright and
          author.

545       ‡a George Heard Hamilton was born June 23, 1910, in
          Pittsburgh, Pennsylvania. He studied at Yale
          University where he received a B.A. in English in
          1932, an M.A. in History in 1934, and a Ph.D. in Art
          History in 1942 ...

545       ‡a Hyman Bradofsky was an amateur journalist active in
          the National Amateur Press Association. In addition
          to publishing the amateur newspaper, The Californian,
          Bradofsky collected examples of amateur journalism,
          as well as materials relating to H.P. Lovecraft and
          Jack London.

110   2   ‡a Monday Evening Concerts of Los Angeles.
245  10   ‡a [Monday Evening Concerts programs].
545       ‡a The Monday Evening Concerts, first known as Evenings
          on the Roof, began in 1939 under the direction of
          Peter Yates. The concerts featured his wife Frances
          Mullen, among others, playing chamber music and other
          experimental works ...
```

520 field: Summary, etc.

Summary notes are narrative, free-text statements of the scope and contents of collections. Details may include forms of materials, dates of subject coverage, and the most significant topics, persons, places, or events. A summary note may be used in lieu of or in addition to a 505 note. If the collection contents are listed in a separate finding aid, use only a 520 note and also make a 555 finding aid note.

```
520        ‡a An ongoing collection of single issues of a variety
              of fanzines, gathered 1995-.

520        ‡a Collection consists of printed and mimeographed
              newsletters, journal issues, brochures, programs,
              announcements, correspondence, meeting minutes, and
              ephemera.

520        ‡a Collection of more than 7,000 items, including
              approximately 6,200 amateur newspapers, periodicals,
              and single publications, the majority of which are
              19th and early 20th century American imprints
              (including approximately 1,000 items that were
              printed in California).

520        ‡a Research and reference files (including
              correspondence). Includes a substantial, but
              incomplete, run of the SFL newsletter (March 1965-
              April 1971), as well as scattered samples of other
              serials on issues of sexual freedom.

520        ‡a Collection of bound and unbound serials related to
              the French Revolution, including several issues of
              Assemblée nationale et commune de France, 10 issues
              of Le journal universel, 5 issues of Auditeur
              national, 26 issues of Mercure de France, and 1 issue
              each of the following: L'observateur; Le courier de
              Paris; and Le flambeau.
```

505 field: Formatted contents note

Formatted contents notes provide a structured method of recording item-level information. Elements may include author, title, edition, date of creation or publication, extent, scale, etc. Assign a number to each item, record it within square brackets in the 505 note, and write it on each item. For materials that lack routine bibliographic indicia, or for large collections of many items, prefer the narrative 520 summary note to the 505 note.

```
505  0    ‡a [1] La mère angot -- [2] Le triboulet -- [3] Revue
              comique -- [4] La flèche -- [5] La charge -- [6] La
              caricature -- [7] Les pamphlets illustrés -- [8] La
              sentinelle -- [9] L'obstacle -- [10] La lutte -- [11]
              Le samperio -- [12] Le cadavre recalcitrant -- [13]
              Le Figaro -- [14] Siège de Paris illustré -- [15] Le
              Gaulois.
```

524 field: Preferred citation

Use to provide a specific citation format for citing the collection.

```
524        ‡a California Ephemera Collection (Collection 200).
           Department of Special Collections, University
           Research Library, University of California, Los
           Angeles.

524    8   ‡a Preferred citation: Hyman Bradofsky Collection of
           Amateur Journalism, A39, The Bancroft Library,
           University of California, Berkeley.
```

541 field: Immediate source of acquisition

Record the immediate source from which the library acquired the collection. Use only for materials acquired as a collection.

```
541    1   ‡a Acquired by exchange from Auburn University; ‡d 1954.

541    0   ‡3 Master copy ‡c Gift; ‡a Mrs. James Hickey; ‡d
           received: 5/22/1989.

541    1   ‡a On permanent loan from the J. Paul Getty Museum.
```

555 field: Cumulative index/finding aids note

Specify the existence of any separate finding aid. An external electronic finding aid may be linked to from this field, if permitted by the local system (see also the 856 field).

```
555    8   ‡a Inventory available in the Wesleyan University
           Department of Special Collections and University
           Archives; ‡c item-level control.

555    8   ‡a Finding aid available in the library and online. ‡u
           http://www.oac.cdlib.org/findaid/ark:/13030/tf967nb3x
           9
```

561 field: Provenance note

Briefly describe any relevant history concerning the ownership of the materials from the time of their creation up until the time of their acquisition by the library.

```
561    1   ‡a The collection belonged to the Earls of Westmoreland
           from 1759-1942.
```

580 field: Linking entry complexity note

Use this note to state the relationship between the materials described and a broader collection of which it is a part. Use only when parts of the collection are being described in separate records (see also the 7XX fields).

```
580          ‡a Forms part of the Margaret Mead Collection.
773   1      ‡t Margaret Mead Collection.
```

6XX fields: Subject headings

Assign subject headings as specific as the collection warrants.

```
245   00   ‡a [Janus Press miscellaneous printed ephemera].
610   20   ‡a Janus Press.
600   10   ‡a Van Vliet, Claire.
650    0   ‡a Artists' books ‡z Vermont ‡z West Burke.
650    0   ‡a Paper, Handmade ‡z Vermont ‡z West Burke.

245   00   ‡a [Italian Communist Party pamphlets].
610   20   ‡a Partito comunista italiano.
651    0   ‡a Italy ‡x Politics and government ‡y 20th century.

245   00   ‡a [Collection of Dutch clandestine periodicals].
520        ‡a Single and selected issues of periodicals printed
              illegally in the Netherlands under the German
              occupation during World War II.
651    0   ‡a Netherlands ‡x History ‡y German occupation, 1940-
              1945 ‡v Periodicals.
650    0   ‡a World War, 1939-1945 ‡x Underground literature ‡z
              Netherlands ‡v Periodicals.

245   00   ‡a [Collection of periodicals and other materials on the
              siege of Paris and the Commune of 1871].
651    0   ‡a Paris (France) ‡x History ‡y Siege, 1870-1871 ‡v
              Periodicals.
651    0   ‡a Paris (France) ‡x History ‡y Commune, 1871 ‡v
              Periodicals.
```

Assign as many subject headings as seem appropriate, remembering that economy in processing may suggest that a reasonable limit be observed.

655 fields: Genre/form headings

Assign as applicable. Prefer terms found in the controlled vocabularies issued by the RBMS Bibliographic Standards Committee; terms from other authorized thesauri (e.g., Art & Architecture Thesaurus Online) may also be used as appropriate. As with subject headings, assign headings as specifically and numerously as the collection and institutional policy warrant.

```
245   00   ‡a [American theater programs of the late 19th and 20th
              centuries].
655    7   ‡a Theater programs ‡z United States ‡y 19th century. ‡2
              rbgenr
655    7   ‡a Theater programs ‡z United States ‡y 20th century. ‡2
              rbgenr
```

```
245  00  ‡a [Fanzine collection].
655   7  ‡a Fanzines. ‡2 rbgenr
655   7  ‡a Periodicals ‡z United States ‡y 20th century. ‡2
            rbgenr
655   7  ‡a Periodicals ‡z United States ‡y 21st century. ‡2
            rbgenr


100   1  ‡a Bradofsky, Hyman, ‡e collector.
245  10  ‡a [Hyman Bradofsky collection of amateur journalism].
655   0  ‡a Amateur journalism.
655   7  ‡a Periodicals ‡z United States ‡y 19th century. ‡2
            rbgenr
655   7  ‡a Periodicals ‡z United States ‡y 20th century. ‡2
            rbgenr
```

7XX fields: Added entries

Types of added entries considered useful for various types of materials include: author/title analytics, government bodies or individual sovereigns (e.g., as authors of the laws), creators of collections, names of collections, etc. In cases where a person or corporate body is both the author or issuing body and the subject of a collection, it may be appropriate to provide both a 6XX subject entry and a 1XX or 7XX entry. If a linking entry complexity note has been used in field 580 to describe the relationship of the collection being cataloged to a larger collection, make an added entry for the larger collection using field 773.

856 field: Electronic location and access

Use to specify the location or means of access to an electronic finding aid prepared for the collection or for other reasons, such as to point to scanned items or digital images selected from the collection. Take special note of the second indicator, which specifies the relationship of the electronic resource being linked to the item described in the record.

```
856  42  ‡3 Finding aid ‡u
            http://lcweb2.loc.gov/ammem/ead/jackson.sgm
```

B5. Additional considerations

B5.1. Lengthy descriptions divided into more than one record. It may be desirable to divide the description of a collection into more than one bibliographic record due to factors such as complexity or length of the description or system limitations on record length. The description may be divided in whatever way is most sensible. For example, the collection may be organized in logical groupings, each of which can be represented in a single record (e.g., pamphlets concerning tobacco consumption, pamphlets encouraging smoking, and pamphlets discouraging smoking). Alternatively, a new record may be started at a logical breaking point, such as with every twentieth item, based on chronology, etc.

When multiple bibliographic records are created for one collection, most data elements will be the same across all records, according to the guidelines discussed above, with the following exceptions:

> *245 field*: ***Title statement.*** Indicate in subfield ‡n or in subfield ‡p, as appropriate, which part of the collection is being represented in the record.

> *260 field*: ***Publication, distribution, etc. (Imprint).*** If the collection is divided based on chronology, include the appropriate range of dates in each record.

> *300 field*: ***Physical description.*** Indicate in the extent statement in the subfield ‡a of each record the number of items represented in the record out of the total number of items in the collection, using terminology appropriate to the material being described.

```
300      ‡a Items 1-40 of 80 in 1 bound volume

300      ‡a Items 41-80 of 80 in 1 bound volume
```

> *5XX fields*: ***Notes.*** With the exception of the 505 contents note (see below), give the same 5XX fields in each record. In addition, indicate in a note in each record that the collection being cataloged is represented by more than one record, and provide references to the other records.

> *505 field*: ***Contents note.*** List in a 505 note only those items described in the particular record. Numbering within contents notes should be consecutive from one record to another.

B5.2. Considerations when adding to collections. Sometimes items are added to collections after initial processing or cataloging has been completed. In such cases, edit or add to the description as necessary, paying particular attention to the following elements:

- ‣ Dates (260 field and fixed fields)
- ‣ Extent (300 field)

‣ Contents (505 and/or 520 field)

‣ Subject and genre/form headings (6XX fields)

‣ Added entries (7XX fields)

Appendix C. Core-Level Records

No general use of this appendix is made for serials.

Appendix D. Minimal-Level Records

D1. Introduction

The elements of description provided in DCRM(S) constitute a full set of information for describing rare materials. This appendix sets out a less than full level of description containing those elements recommended as a minimum for effective description of early printed serials and other rare materials.

Libraries most often turn to minimal-level cataloging for rare materials in response to a need to create item-level records for large backlogs of uncataloged materials with the least amount of time and effort possible. These guidelines are provided in response to such needs. Their purpose is not to promote the use of DCRM(S) minimal-level cataloging, but rather to provide a usable standard for those institutions wishing to adopt it.

D2. Application

Catalogers may apply the minimal-level standard to any rare materials described using DCRM(S). DCRM(S) minimal-level records are especially appropriate when faithful and accurate descriptions are desirable, the provision of subject and other access points is not necessarily important, and abridged transcriptions and fewer notes are acceptable.

A minimal-level cataloging policy is best kept simple. Complex rules for omitting or shortening a variety of record elements would require catalogers to devote time to learning these new rules, thereby eliminating a portion of the intended gains in time and expense. In addition, tampering with the full description provided by DCRM(S) areas 0-6 and 8 would negate the very purpose of using DCRM(S) for description of rare materials. The conclusion then is that eliminating notes accomplishes much of the purpose of minimal-level cataloging because it saves considerable time while not unduly limiting access. Bibliographic records following this approach will, in most cases, still identify the serials being described and distinguish them from similar editions or issues.

D3. Elements of the bibliographic record

D3.1. Follow the rules in DCRM(S) areas 0-6 and 8. Abridge the description wherever possible as allowed by the rules. It is not necessary to make the notes usually considered required.

D3.2. *Optionally*, add any additional elements in accordance with institutional policy. In particular, consider adding one or more of the following, each of which can significantly enhance the value of minimal-level DCRM(S) records for identifying rare materials:

- references to published descriptions in standard bibliographies, particularly when the source cited provides more detailed information than the minimal-level bibliographic record (see 7B17)

- the required notes called for in DCRM(S) (a complete list of required notes may be found in the Index under "Required notes")

- one or more local notes describing provenance, copy numbering, imperfections, binding, or any other information that will allow the bibliographic record to describe the particular copy in hand with sufficient precision to indicate the institution's ownership of that particular copy

- optional notes based on reliable dealers' descriptions accompanying the item being described

D3.3. Minimal-level cataloging policies often eliminate or simplify additional areas of the bibliographic record such as subject headings, classification, or other access points. This appendix does not address such questions, but users of DCRM(S) may also wish to streamline these areas according to local needs, taking into consideration the effect that such policies will have on special files for printers, binders, bindings, genres/forms, provenance, and the like.

APPENDIX E. VARIATIONS REQUIRING A NEW RECORD

E1. Major changes

E1.1. Make a new bibliographic record if a major change occurs in the title proper of a serial.

E1.2. In general, consider as a major change in a title proper the addition, deletion, change, or reordering of any of the first five words (the first six words if the title begins with an article) unless the change belongs to one or more of the categories listed in Minor changes (see Appendix E2).

E1.3. Consider also as a major change in a title proper the addition, deletion, or change of any word after the first five words (the first six words if the title begins with an article) that changes the meaning of the title or indicates a different subject matter.

E1.4. Consider also as a major change in a title proper a change in a corporate body name given anywhere in the title if it is a different corporate body.

E1.5. Make a new bibliographic record if any of the following conditions arises, even if the title proper of the serial remains the same:

△ if the heading for a corporate body under which a serial is entered changes

△ if the main entry for a serial is under a personal or corporate heading and the person or body named in that heading is no longer responsible for the serial

△ if the main entry for a serial is under a uniform title (see AACR2 25.5B) with a corporate heading as a qualifier and the corporate heading changes or the body named in that heading is no longer responsible for the serial

E2. Minor changes

E2.1. Do not make a new bibliographic record in response to minor changes in the title proper of a serial. Rather, make a note in the existing record as appropriate (see 7B4.3). Make an added entry (see Appendix F) under any variant form considered necessary for access.

E2.2. In general, consider the following to be a minor change in a title proper:

- a difference in the representation of a word or words anywhere in the title (e.g., one spelling vs. another; abbreviated word or sign or symbol vs. spelled-out form; arabic numeral(s) vs. roman numeral(s); numbers or dates vs. spelled-out form; hyphenated words vs. unhyphenated words; one-word compounds vs. two-word compounds, whether hyphenated or not; an acronym or initialism vs. full form; or a change in grammatical form (e.g., singular vs. plural))

- the addition, deletion, or change of articles, prepositions, or conjunctions anywhere in the title

- a difference involving the name of the same corporate body and elements of its hierarchy or their grammatical connection anywhere in the title (e.g., the addition, deletion, or rearrangement of the name of the same corporate body or the substitution of a variant form)

- the addition, deletion, or change of punctuation, including initialisms and letters with separating punctuation vs. those without separating punctuation, anywhere in the title

- a different order of titles when the title is given in more than one language in the chief source of information, provided that the title chosen as title proper still appears as a parallel title

- the addition, deletion, or change of words anywhere in the title that link the title to the numbering

- two or more titles proper used on different issues of a serial according to a regular pattern

- the addition to, deletion from, or change in the order of words in a list anywhere in a title, provided that there is no significant change in the subject matter

- the addition or deletion anywhere in the title of words that indicate the type of resource such as "magazine," "journal," or "newsletter" or their equivalents in other languages

E2.3. In case of doubt, consider the change to be a minor change.

Descriptive Cataloging of Rare Materials (Serials)

APPENDIX F. TITLE ACCESS POINTS

F1. Introduction

Title access plays an important role in enabling users to identify and locate special collections materials. While some title access will be handled by controlled forms, this appendix lists specific situations, commonly encountered by rare materials catalogers, in which the provision of uncontrolled title access points is likely to be useful.

This appendix is not intended as an exhaustive list of all instances in which uncontrolled title access points may be made. Use judgment in determining which forms of access will be most useful for the item in hand. In general, do not include access points that duplicate normalized forms of existing title access points (e.g., the title proper, a uniform title). Take the indexing capabilities of the institution's local system into consideration when determining whether the additional access points are needed.

F2. Rules relevant to the provision of title access points

The list is presented in DCRM(S) rule number order. Title access points considered optional are labeled as such.

0B1. Title proper

Provide access for the entire title proper exactly as transcribed, disregarding initial articles as required by filing rules.

0F1.1. Title proper in nonroman script

If nonroman text has been transcribed within the first five words of the title proper, provide additional title access for a romanized version of the title proper using the *ALA-LC Romanization Tables.*

> *Transcription:*
> Журнал геофизики и метеорологии
>
> *Additional title access:*
> Zhurnal geofiziki i meteorologii

0G2.2. Title proper with converted letters i/j or u/v

If any of the first five words in the title proper contains a letter **i/j/u/v** that has been converted to uppercase or lowercase according to a pattern of usage that follows pre-modern spelling conventions, provide additional title access for the form of the title proper that corresponds to modern orthography (i.e., using **i** and **u** for vowels, **j** and **v** for consonants, and **w** for consonantal **vv**).

If it differs from title access points already provided, also provide title access for the form of the title proper that corresponds to the graphical appearance of the letters in the source, converting the letters **i/j/u/v** into uppercase or lowercase without regard for the pattern of usage in the serial being described.

> *Source:*
>
> VVeekly memorials for the ingenious , or, an account of books lately set
>   forth in several languages with other accounts relating to arts and
>   sciences

> *Transcription:*
> ```
> VVeekly memorials for the ingenious, or, An account of books
>    lately set forth in several languages : with other accounts
>    relating to arts and sciences
> ```

> *Additional title access (normalized modern):*
> ```
> Weekly memorials for the ingenious, or, An account of books
>    lately set forth in several languages : with other accounts
>    relating to arts and sciences
> ```

0G3.7. Title proper containing characters as substitutes for letters (Optional)

If a title proper contains hyphens or other characters as substitutes for letters, and the meaning of the characters is known, provide additional access to the decoded form of the title.

> *Source:*
>
> The r -- l register: with annotations by another hand

> *Transcription:*
> ```
> The r---l register : with annotations by another hand
> ```
> *Optional note:* The r---l register is The royal register

> *Additional title access:*
> ```
> Royal register
> ```

0G4.2. Title proper with inserted spacing

If any spacing has been inserted in the transcription of the first five words of the title proper, provide additional title access for the form of title with the words closed up.

Source:
The DUTCHSPY

Transcription:
The Dutch spy

Additional title access:
Dutchspy

0G4.3. Title proper with variant spellings

If any variant or archaic spellings have been transcribed in the first five words of the title proper, provide additional title access for the form of title with spacing inserted between the words.

Source:
Newhampshire & Vermont ALMANAC

Transcription:
Newhampshire & Vermont almanac

Additional title access:
New Hampshire & Vermont almanac

0G7.1. Title proper with corrected misprint

If any of the first five words in the title proper contains a misprint that has been corrected in the transcription through the insertion of [i.e. ...], provide additional title access for the form of title proper as it appears in the source, without the correction. In addition, provide title access for the form of title as if it had been printed correctly.

Source:
Englands remembrancer of Lodons integritie

Transcription:
Englands remembrancer of Lodons [i.e. Londons] integritie

Additional title access (without interpolation):
```
Englands remembrancer of Lodons integritie
```

Additional title access (with correct spelling):
```
Englands remembrancer of Londons integritie
```

If any of the first five words in the title proper contains a misprint that has been qualified in the transcription by the insertion of **[sic]**, provide additional title access for the form of title proper without the **[sic]**. In addition, provide title access for the form of title as if it had been printed correctly.

Source:
Police regulations for the Amry of the District of Eastern Arkansas

Transcription:
```
Police regulations for the Amry [sic] of the District of Eastern
   Arkansas
```

Additional title access (without interpolation):
```
Police regulations for the Amry of the District of Eastern
   Arkansas
```

Additional title access (with correct spelling):
```
Police regulations for the Army of the District of Eastern
   Arkansas
```

0G7.1. Title proper with non-standard orthography (Optional)

If the title proper contains words spelled according to older or non-standard orthographic conventions, provide additional title access for the title spelled according to modern orthography. If orthographical variations appear on different issues of the serial itself, see 1B7.

0G7.2. Title proper with approximated letters

If any of the first five words in the title proper contains two letters used to approximate a third letter, provide additional title access for the form of title proper with the letters transcribed as set.

Source:
Anrveisung Zu der Geographia Oder Beschreibung des Erdbodens

Transcription:
```
Anweisung zu der Geographia, oder, Beschreibung des Erdbodens
```

Additional title access:
```
Anrveisung zu der Geographia, oder, Beschreibung des Erdbodens
```

0G10. Title proper with initials, etc. (Optional)

If the title proper contains initials, initialisms, or acronyms with internal spaces, provide additional title access for the title with the spaces closed up. Conversely, if the title proper contains initials, initialisms, or acronyms without internal spaces, provide title access for the title with the spaces inserted.

1B1.1. Title proper with transposed elements (Optional)

If an element appearing before the title proper on the title page has been transposed, provide additional title access for the title inclusive of the preceding element. If the preceding element has not been transposed, so that the title proper includes it, provide additional title access for the title without the preceding element.

1B1.3. Title appearing in both full form and in form of an initialism or acronym in the chief source of information

If a title appears in full and in the form of an initialism or acronym in the chief source of information, provide additional title access for the initialism or acronym transcribed as other title information.

Source:
BLM Bonniers litterära magasin

Transcription:
```
Bonniers litterära magasin : BLM
```

Additional title access:
```
BLM
```

1B3.1. Title proper inclusive of an alternative title (Optional)

Provide additional title access for an alternative title.

1B5. Title proper with supplementary or section title (Optional)

Provide additional title access for a title that is supplementary to, or a section of, another work when both titles, whether or not grammatically separable, are recorded together as the title proper. If the supplement or section title is a title such as "Supplement" or "Série B," however, and so is indistinctive and dependent for its meaning on the main title, generally do not provide additional access.

1B7. Change in title proper

If a minor change in title proper occurs, provide additional title access for the subsequent title.

1C. Parallel titles (Optional)

Provide additional title access for a parallel title.

1D2. Transposed other title information

Provide additional title access for transposed other title information.

1E14. Phrases about notes, appendixes, etc. (Optional)

Provide additional title access for phrases concerning notes, appendixes, etc., if the phrase is distinctive and the additional access seems useful.

6B1. Title proper of series (Optional)

Provide access for the series title proper exactly as it appears in the serial, unless title access is provided using a uniform series title.

7B4-7B5. Title variants and other titles

Provide additional access for cover titles, added title page titles, caption titles, half titles, running titles, spine titles, distinctive titles, volume title page titles, individual issue titles, and significant other title information. Provide additional access for any of these titles that change in subsequent issues.

7B13. Titles of accompanying material (Optional)

Provide additional access for any separate title on accompanying material deemed useful.

7B22. Copy-specific titles (Optional)

Provide additional access for copy-specific titles, such as a binder's title.

Appendix G. Early Letter Forms and Symbols

G1. Introduction

This appendix provides guidance for transcription of archaic letter and character forms, including marks of punctuation, and archaic conventions of contraction. Although this appendix cannot be exhaustive, it is intended to provide sufficient guidance for the most common occurrences, and to give a basis for judgment in ambiguous situations. For transcription of characters commonly found in signature statements that cannot be reproduced using available typographical facilities, see DCRM(B) 7B9.2.

G2. Early letter forms and symbols

According to the instructions for transcription in rule 0G1.1, earlier forms of letters and symbols are converted to their modern forms.

Early letter forms and symbols				
Source	*Transcription*	*Example*	*Transcription of example*	*Notes*
ꝺ	d	Dethe	dethe	
ij ÿ	ij	alijs ooghelijck	alijs ooghelijck	Ligatured italic **ij** may look like **ÿ**
k	k			Typical in early French signatures
cIɔ Iɔ	M D	cIɔIɔccv	MDCCV	Inverted **C** used to form Roman numeral **M** or **D** is called an apostrophus
ꝛ ꝛ	r	foꝛ	for	
ſ ſ ſ	s	refuſe	refuse	Long **s** (an **f** has a crossbar on the stem; the bar on a long **s**, if present, extends from one side only)

ſ ß ß ß	ss	deſ	dess	
ß	sz	Deſz	desz	Long **s** and **z** are spaced normally, no ligature
ȝ	-	West-Riding	West-Riding	
o	o	můß	mŭss	
e	..	bůͤche	Büche	Superscript **e** functioning as an umlaut
& & ⁊ ꝛ	&	ꝛc.	&c.	

G3. Early contractions

According to the instructions for transcription in rule 0G8.2, symbols of contraction used in continuance of the manuscript tradition are expanded to their full form, with cataloger-supplied letters or words enclosed in square brackets. The values of many contractions are dependent on context, with the most common values provided here.

Early contractions				
Source	*Transcription*	*Example*	*Transcription of example*	*Notes*
◌̄	[missing letter(s)]	cōſummatū dñs	co[n]summatu[m] D[omi]n[u]s	Over a vowel, usually **n** or **m**; over a consonant, often replaces several letters
ę	[ae]	hęc	h[ae]c	
xp̄s	[Christus]			A contraction using both Greek and Latin letters
ꝯ	[con]	ꝯcoꝛᵃ	[con]cor[di]a	

ꝫ ꝫ	[es] [ius] [us]	ſtatutꝫ roſſꝫ cuꝫ eiꝫ	statut[es] Ross[es] cu[ius] ei[us]	A highly versatile symbol; see also, for example, "[habet]," "[que]," "[scilicet]" and "[sed]" below
ƀꝫ	[habet]			
ƀ	[hoc]			
ꝑ	[per] [par]	ſuꝑ ꝑticulari⁹	su[per] [par]ticulari[bus]	
ꝓ	[pro]	ꝓpter	[pro]pter	
ꝑ̇	[pri]	ꝑ̇ma	[pri]ma	
ꝙ̃	[quam]	vnꝙ̃	vn[quam]	
q̃	[quan]	q̃tum	[quan]tum	
ꝗ ꝗꝫ ꝗ;	[que]	quoꝗꝫ herculeæꝗꝫ quoſꝗ;	quo[que] Herculeae[que] quos[que]	
ꝗ̇	[qui]	ꝗ̇b⁹	[qui]b[us]	
ꝗ̃	[quia]			
ꝗ̊	[quo]			
qꝺ qꝺ	[quod]			
ꝛc̃.	[recta]			
ꝝ ꝶ	[rum]	quoꝝ libroꝶ	quo[rum] libro[rum]	
ſcꝫ	[scilicet]			
ƀꝫ	[sed]			
ẏ	[th]	ẏͤ ẏͭ	[the] [that]	When **y** is used to represent the Old English/Icelandic character **þ** [thorn], enclose **th** plus additional letters in square brackets.

z	[ur]	naſcunt*ᶻ*	nascunt[ur]	
9	[us] [bus]	**reb⁹** **pticulari⁹**	reb[us] [par]ticulari[bus]	Superscript; a similar character at baseline represents "[con]"
ꝟ	[ver]	**ꝟtuoſo**	[ver]tuoso	

G4. Letters i/j and u/v

G4.1. Historical background. Some knowledge of the history of printing as it applies to the letters **i/j** and **u/v** is helpful when applying the provisions of 0G2.2.

Until the early seventeenth century, the standard Latin alphabet contained 23 letters. The letters we know as **i** and **j** were considered different minuscule shapes (or graphs) of the same letter, as were the letters **u** and **v**. The letter **w** was not part of the standard Latin alphabet. A printer's choice for the **u** graph in preference to the **v** graph (or the **i** to the **j**) depended on its placement in a word and was governed by convention. Conventions varied somewhat from printer to printer, but often reflected national and regional preferences. While there were variant graphs for lowercase letters, in the pre-modern distribution there was only one graph for each of these letters used as capitals: **I** (with the gothic form resembling a modern **J**), and **V** (with the gothic form resembling a modern **U**). For example, **𝕵𝖆𝖈𝖔𝖇** = Iacob; **𝖀𝖓𝖘𝖕𝖔𝖙𝖙𝖊𝖉** = Vnspotted (capitalized as the first word of a title).

The dominant patterns in use before the seventeenth century were:

- **i** used in the initial, medial, and final position, without signifying vocalic or consonantal use; e.g., iustice (modern form: justice)

- **j** used in the medial or final position only after a preceding **i** (more typical on the European continent), signifying vocalic use; e.g., commentarij (modern form: commentarii)

- **u** used in the initial, medial or final position, without signifying vocalic or consonantal use; e.g., oeuures (modern form: oeuvres)

- **v** used in the initial position, without signifying vocalic or consonantal use; e.g., vtilita (modern form: utilita)

- **I** used in all positions, without signifying vocalic or consonantal use; e.g., Iuan (modern form: Juan)

‣ **V** used in all positions, without signifying vocalic or consonantal use; e.g., Vrsprung (modern form: Ursprung)

A gradual shift took place over time, from the late fifteenth century through the middle of the seventeenth century, with **U/u** coming to phonetically signify a vowel and **V/v** to signify a consonant, regardless of case or position in the word. Likewise with **i** and **j**, although the shift was more irregular, with **I/i** coming to phonetically signify a vowel and **J/j** a consonant. In the modern 26-letter Latin alphabet, **i** and **j** and **u** and **v** are all considered separate letters.

G4.2. Transcription. As instructed in rule 0G2.2, when the rules for capitalization require converting **i/j** or **u/v** to uppercase or lowercase,[21] the cataloger is to follow the pattern of usage in the serial being described. Establish the pattern of usage by examining text in the same typeface (i.e., roman, italic, or gothic) in the serial being described. Identify examples of **i**, **j**, **u**, and **v** having the same function (vowel or consonant) and same relative position (appearing in initial, medial, or final positions) as the letters to be converted. Begin by examining the remainder of the title page and then, if necessary, proceed to examine the body of the text in other parts of the book in the same typeface. If the pattern of usage cannot be determined within a reasonable amount of time, use this conversion table as a solution of last resort.

Uppercase letter to be converted	*Lowercase conversion*
I (vowel or consonant) anywhere in word[22]	i
II at end of word	ij
II elsewhere in word	ii
V (vowel or consonant) at beginning of word	v
V (vowel or consonant) elsewhere in word	u
VV representing single letter[23]	vv

---

[21] An uppercase **J** or **U** in the source signals a modern distribution, in which **i** and **j** are functioning as separate letters, as are **u** and **v**, requiring no special consideration while converting case.

[22] Do not convert a final uppercase **I** meant to represent an **ii** ending (see DCRM(B) 0G2.3).

Lowercase letter to be converted	Uppercase conversion
i (vowel or consonant) anywhere in word	I
j (vowel or consonant) anywhere in word	I
u (vowel or consonant) anywhere in word	V
v (vowel or consonant) anywhere in word	V
vv representing single letter[23]	VV

G5. Letter w

G5.1. Historical background. The representation of the letter **w** is not to be confused with the developments of the **u/v** graphs. The **w** graph was part of the standard alphabet for Germanic languages. Most early printing was in Latin, shifting gradually to include a greater proportion of vernacular languages throughout Europe. **W** and **w** must have been scanty in cases of roman type, and they appear to have been frequently exhausted when setting text in Dutch, English, or German. When that happened, compositors usually did one of two things: used **VV** or **vv** to stand in for **W** or **w**, or permanently altered **V** or **v** type pieces—achieved by filing or shaving one of the serifs, often the right serif on the left piece—so that the two type pieces would sit closely together in the forme, thereby more closely resembling a **w**. In early German texts, printers sometimes used a curved **r** followed by a **v** to approximate a **w**.

G5.2. Transcription. When **VV** and **vv** graphs have been used to represent the single letter **W** or **w**, transcribe them as **VV** or **vv** as appropriate. When there is clear evidence of the filing of one or both pieces of type showing the intention of creating the **W** or **w** graph, transcribe as **W** or **w**, making an explanatory note, if considered important. In cases of doubt, transcribe as **VV** and **vv**. When separate **rv** graphs have been used by the printer to approximate the single letter **W** or **w**, transcribe as **W** or **w**, making an explanatory note, if considered important (see 0G7.2).

---

[23] This must be distinguished from **VV** or **vv** as a combination of a vowel and a consonant as in the examples VVLT or vvlt (vult, "he wants") and VVA or vva (uva, "grape").

Forms of W				
Source	*Transcription*	*Example*	*Transcription of example*	*Notes*
VV	vv	VVhole	vvhole	
W	w	WHOLE	whole	
ᛉv	w	ᛉveyße	weysse	

Appendix H. Individual and Special Issues of Serials

Apply these guidelines when creating a bibliographic record for an individual or special issue of a serial, whether or not also creating a record for the serial as a whole. Individual and special issues may be cataloged as monographs and related to the serial as a whole.

H1. Bibliographic level

The bibliographic level for an issue of a serial is **m** (monograph), just as it is for an individual part of a multipart monograph cataloged separately.

H2. Body of the description

H2.1. General rule

Formulate the body of the description according to the rules in DCRM(B). Transcribe information in the form and order in which it is presented in the source, unless instructed otherwise by specific rules (see 0G).

H2.2. Issues with distinctive titles

If the issue has a distinctive title, transcribe that title in the title and statement of responsibility area.

H2.3. Issues without distinctive titles

H2.3.1. If the issue has no distinctive title, transcribe the title of the serial and the numbering of the issue (including numeric and/or chronological designations) in the title and statement of responsibility area.

```
245  04  ‡a The post boy. ‡n Numb. 2436, from Thursday December
             21 to Saturday December 23, 1710.

245  04  ‡a The American printer. ‡p Franklin bi-centennial
             number. ‡n January 20, 1923.

245  14  ‡a The foundling hospital for wit : ‡b intended for the
             reception and preservation of such brats of wit and
             humour whose parents chuse to drop them. ‡n Number
             III, to be continued occasionally / ‡c by Timothy
             Silence, Esq.
```

H2.3.2. If the issue numbering appears at the head of title, transpose it and make a note indicating the transposition (see 1B5).

H2.3.3. If the issue numbering appears following a statement of responsibility, transcribe it as a subsequent statement of responsibility.

H3. Relating individual issues to the serial as a whole

H3.1. General rule

To relate the description of an individual issue to the description of the serial as a whole and to provide organized access to the records in the catalog, make a series added entry using the uniform title for the serial. Apply AACR2 and LCRI in formulating the uniform title.

H3.2. Issues with distinctive titles

For access to the serial title on a monographic record for an issue that has a distinctive title, give a simple series statement (440) if the serial title will be traced in the form in which it appears on the piece. If the serial title appearing on the piece is not in the form in which it will be traced, give an uncontrolled series statement (490) with a series added entry (8XX).

```
245  02  ‡a A book of humorous limericks / ‡c edited by Clement
             Wood.
440   0  ‡a Little blue book ; ‡v no. 1018

245  00  ‡a Earthquake potential in Colorado.
490   1  ‡a Bulletin / Colorado Geological Survey, Department of
             Natural Resources, State of Colorado ; ‡v 43
830   0  ‡a Bulletin (Colorado Geological Survey) ; ‡v 43.
```

H3.3. Issues without distinctive titles

For access to the serial title on a monographic record for an issue that does not have a distinctive title, give a series added entry (8XX).

```
245  14  ‡a The foundling hospital for wit : ‡b intended for the
             reception and preservation of such brats of wit and
             humour whose parents chuse to drop them. ‡n Number
             III, to be continued occasionally / ‡c by Timothy
             Silence, Esq.
800   1  ‡a Silence, Timothy. ‡t Foundling hospital for wit ; ‡v
             no. 3.

245  00  ‡a Hoopoe. ‡n Spring 1991, issue no. 7.
830   0  ‡a Hoopoe ; ‡v issue no. 7.

245  00  ‡a Almanacco anti letterario Bompiani. ‡n 1937-XV.
830   0  ‡a Almanacco anti letterario Bompiani ; ‡v 1937.
```

H3.4. Issue numbering

H3.4.1. General rule. Transcribe issue numbering (including numeric and/or chronological designations) in full in the descriptive areas, but standardize issue numbering in the added entry for the serial. This will provide both the accurate representation of individual issues as well as an organized display of sequential issues within the catalog.

```
245  04   ‡a The post boy ‡n Numb. 2436, from Thursday December 21
             to Saturday December 23, 1710.
830   0   ‡a Post boy (London, England) ; ‡v no. 2436.
```

H3.4.2. Chronological designation only. If the issue has only a chronological designation, use "year month day" as the standardized form of the chronological designation in the access point.

```
245  04   ‡a The English Lucian, or, Weekly discoveries of the
             witty intrigues, comical passages, and remarkable
             transactions in town and country with reflections on
             the vices and vanities of the times. ‡n Friday the
             17th of January, 1698.
830   0   ‡a English Lucian ; ‡v 1698 Jan. 17.
```

H4. Relating special issues to the serial as a whole

H4.1. Special issues

A special issue of a serial usually covers a particular topic. It may have a distinctive title or it may simply be called "special issue" or the equivalent. Some special issues are published within the numbering system of a serial; others are published outside the numbering system of a serial. The statement identifying a special issue as such may be presented formally in the publication or it may presented informally (e.g., embedded in text).

H4.2. Special issues outside the numbering of a serial

If the special issue is outside the numbering of the serial, relate the monograph to the serial title by giving a uniform title added entry (7XX) for the serial. If the statement identifying the special issue as such is not presented formally, give the information in a note in order to justify the added entry.

```
245  00   ‡a Champions in the sun : ‡b a special issue of
             California history, the magazine of the California
             Historical Society / ‡c Frances Ring, guest editor.
730   0   ‡a California history.
```

```
245  04  ‡a The trout season of 1883 : ‡b the trout of American
             waters.
500       ‡a "The American angler. A weekly journal of fish and
             fishing. Special issue for the trout season of
             1883"--P. [1].
730   0  ‡a American angler (New York, N.Y. : 1881)
```

H4.3. Special issues within the numbering of a serial

Special issues that are published within the numbering of the serial are related to the serial by means of a simple series statement (440) if the serial title will be traced in the form in which it appears on the piece. If the serial title appearing on the piece is not in the form in which it will be traced, give an uncontrolled series statement (490) with a series added entry (8XX). If the statement identifying the special issue as such is not presented formally, give the information in a note in order to justify the added entry.

```
100  1   ‡a Berrigan, Ted.
245  10  ‡a Carrying a torch / ‡c Ted Berrigan.
500      ‡a "Published as Clown war 22 in January 1980"--P. [2]
            of cover.
830   0  ‡a Clown war ; ‡v 22.


245  00  ‡a Chelsea retrospective 1958-1983.
490  1   ‡a Chelsea, ‡x 0009-2185 ; ‡v 42/43
500      ‡a "25th anniversary, 1958/1982"--P. [4] of cover.
830   0  ‡a Chelsea (New York, N.Y.) ; ‡v 42/43.


245  04  ‡a The black press : ‡b special issue.
490  1   ‡a Harvard journal of Afro-American affairs ; ‡v volume
            2, number 2, 1971
830   0  ‡a Harvard journal of Afro-American affairs ; ‡v v. 2,
            no. 2.
```

H5. Relating separately published monographs to the serial as a whole

Serial issues with distinctive titles may also have been published separately as monographs. Do not treat these monographs as part of the serial. When cataloging such a monograph, make a note to indicate that the title was also published as an issue of the serial. Give a uniform title added entry (7XX) for the serial.

```
245  04  ‡a The forbidden stitch : ‡b an Asian American women's
            anthology / ‡c edited by Shirley Geok-lin Lim, Mayumi
            Tsutakawa, Margarita Donnelly (managing editor).
500      ‡a "Also published as vol. 11 #2&3 of Calyx, a journal
            of art and literature by women"--Half-title verso.
730   0  ‡a Calyx (Corvallis, Or.)
```

```
245  04   ‡a The black revolution : ‡b an Ebony special issue.
500       ‡a "First published as a special issue of Ebony magazine
              August, 1969"--T.p. verso.
730  0    ‡a Ebony (Chicago, Ill.)
```

H6. Linking records for individual issues to the serial record

Optionally, when cataloging an individual issue of a serial, provide a linking entry between the record for the individual issue and the record for the serial as a whole by means of a host item entry (773):

```
773  0    ‡a Silence, Timothy. ‡t Foundling hospital for wit. ‡g
              No. 3
```

```
773  0    ‡a Post boy (London, England). ‡g No. 2436
```

APPENDIX J. REISSUED SERIALS

J1. Introduction

J1.1. This appendix offers guidance in the cataloging of reissued[24] serials. A reissue of a serial is published subsequent to the original serial and may:

- have the same title as the original or a new title

- have the same numbering as the original or carry a new series of numbers

- be published in the same place as the original or in a different place

- be published by the same publisher, distributor, etc., as the original or by a different publisher, distributor, etc.

- be published all at once in a single volume, or in several volumes or numbered parts

- be published serially over time, although usually a shorter period of time than it took for the publication of the original

- physically resemble the original, or be reprinted in a different format

- have issues that run together so that one number succeeds another without break in the text, or may reproduce the style and appearance of the original issues

- cumulate issues variously

- have the same content as the original or abridge, rearrange, or add content

J1.2. Consider a reissued serial to be a republication if it preserves the original text and the original order of the text (see J2). Consider a reissued serial to be a new serial if the text of the original serial has been substantially changed, abridged, or rearranged (see J3). Consider the reissue of a single issue or selected number of issues to be a monograph (see J4).

J1.3. Use reference sources to verify information when needed to determine whether or not a serial is a reissue. In case of doubt, assume that it is not a reissue.

---

[24] "Reissued" refers to republished or reprinted serials. It does not refer to facsimile reproductions.

J2. Republication of a serial

J2.1. General rule

Consider a reissued serial to be a republication if it preserves the complete text and order of the original. Variations in size, number of issues or volumes, designations, the addition of a new volume title page with new designations, and/or additional introductory matter, indexes, illustrations, etc., are common with such reissues.

Catalog the reissue according to the rules in DCRM(S). Base the description on the reissue. Give information about the original serial, if known, in a note (see 7B7.9). For guidance in MARC 21 encoding, see J2.6.

J2.2. Uniform titles

If the original serial has a uniform title, use the identical uniform title to collocate the reissue with the original serial.

Original:

```
130  0    ‡a Adventurer (London, England : 1752)
260       ‡a London : ‡b Printed for J. Payne, at Pope's Head, in
             Paternoster-row, ‡c MDCCLII-MDCCLIV [1752-1754]
```

Reissue:

```
130  0    ‡a Adventurer (London, England : 1752)
260       ‡a London : ‡b Printed by Charles Green Say, for J.
             Payne, at Pope's Head, in Pater-Noster Row, ‡c
             MDCCLIV [1754]
```

Optionally, add the date of publication of the reissue, or the date of the first volume or issue of the reissue, to the uniform title in order to distinguish it from the original and/or other reissues.

```
130  0    ‡a Adventurer (London, England : 1752). ‡f 1754.
```

J2.3. Numbering

If a reissued serial has a volume title page, give the designation that appears on the volume title page (see 3G). For a reissued serial published in a different number of volumes than the original serial publication, record the number of physical volumes and make a note recording the designations that appear on the individual issues (see 5B2). If it is not feasible to record the designations of each volume, record the designations of the first and/or last volumes.

Example: Serial originally published in 140 numbers. Reissued in 3 volumes.

Original:

```
300        ‡a 140 v. ; ‡c 48 cm (fol.)
362  0     ‡a Number I (Tuesday, November 7, 1752)-number CXL
              (Saturday, March 9, 1754)
```

Reissue:

```
300        ‡a 3 v. ; ‡c 23 cm (8vo)
362  0     ‡a Volume the first-volume the third.
500        ‡a Individual issues have designations: v. 1: Numb. I
              (Tuesday, November 7, 1752)-numb. XLVII (Tuesday,
              April 17, 1753); v. 2: Numb. XLVIII (Saturday, April
              21, 1753)-numb. XCII (Saturday, September 22, 1753);
              v. 3: Numb. XCIII (Tuesday, September 25, 1753)-numb.
              CXL (Saturday, March 9, 1754).
```

J2.4. Series

Transcribe a series statement if the reissue is published as part of a series.

```
440  0     ‡a Harrison's British classicks ; ‡v v. 1
```

```
440  0     ‡a Arno series of contemporary art ; ‡v no. 3
```

J2.5. Notes

Make a note citing details of the original serial. Include information about the reissue not covered elsewhere.

```
580        ‡a Reissue. Originally published weekly as: The
              craftsman. London, 1726-1727.
```

J2.6. MARC 21 encoding

FIELD	NAME	COMMENTS
008/6	Type of date/Publication status	Code for publication status
008/7-14	Dates	Code for coverage
008/15-17	Place of publication, production, or execution	Code for place of reissue publisher, distributor, etc.
008/18-19	Frequency/Regularity	Code for the reissue (usually **u/u**)
008/21	Type of continuing resource	Code for the original
008/23	Form of item	Code as **blank**
1XX	Main entries	Give as applicable; use same uniform title as original, if original has one
245	Title statement	Base on the reissue title page
250	Edition statement	Base on the reissue
260	Publication, distribution, etc.	Base on the reissue
300	Physical description	Base on the reissue
310	Current publication frequency	Base on the reissue
362	Dates of publication and/or sequential designation	Base on the reissue
4XX/8XX	Series statements	Give only if reissue is issued in series
580	Linking entry complexity note	Reissue note - give details of original (frequency, place, and name of publisher, distributor, etc.) as appropriate
775	Other edition entry	Give the linking entry for the original serial (*optional*)

J3. Reissue as a new serial

J3.1. General rule

Consider the following reissues to be new serials, rather than republications:

> ‣ a serial reissued serially, with new designations and/or a new frequency

> ‣ a serial reissued with substantial changes to the content (i.e., the text has

been changed, abridged, cumulated, added to substantially, and/or rearranged, etc.)

In such cases, do not refer to J2.6 for guidance. Catalog the reissue according to the rules in DCRM(S). Base the description on the reissue. Give information about the original serial in a note (see 7B7.9), with corresponding linking entry, if considered important.

J3.2. Uniform titles

Distinguish the resulting new serial from the original serial by creating an appropriate uniform title for the new serial.

Original serial:

```
130  0   ‡a Boys of England (London, England : Weekly)
362  1   ‡a Began 24/27 Nov. 1866; ceased in 1893.
500      ‡a Description based on: Vol. VIII, no. 190 (July 4,
             1870); title from caption.
```

Weekly reissue:

```
130  0   ‡a Boys of England (London, England : Weekly : Reissue)
362  1   ‡a Began 20 Apr. 1874; ceased 14 Apr. 1885.
580      ‡a Reissue of 574 issues in 22 volumes. Originally
             printed weekly: London : Printed and published for
             the proprietor, E.J. Brett ..., 1866-1893.
500      ‡a Description based on: Vol. III, no. 78 (October 5,
             1875); title from caption.
```

Monthly reissue:

```
130  0   ‡a Boys of England (London, England : Monthly)
362  1   ‡a Began in 1866?
362  0   ‡a -Vol. LXVI, part 392 (July 1899)
500      ‡a Monthly cumulation of weekly numbers.
500      ‡a Description based on: Vol. L, part 295 (June 1891);
             title from cover.
```

J4. Reissue as a monograph

Catalog the following as monographs:

 ‣ reissue of a single issue (see Appendix H)

 ‣ reissue of a selected number of issues

 ‣ reissue of bibliographically unrelated serials, with title page

Catalog the reissue according to the rules in DCRM(B).

J5. Examples

J5.1. Republication of a serial with a new volume title page

a. The spectator

```
130  0   ‡a Spectator (London, England : 1711)
245 14   ‡a The spectator.
250      ‡a New edition, carefully corrected from the originals.
260      ‡a London : ‡b Printed for J. Bumpus, Holborn-Bars,
            Sharpe and Son, Priestley, Christie; Jennings ...
            [and forty-seven others], ‡c 1819.
300      ‡a 8 v. ; ‡c 23 cm (8vo)
362  0   ‡a Vol. I-Vol. VIII.
500      ‡a Individual issues have designations: v. 1: No. 1
            (Thursday, March 1, 1710-11)-no. 80 (Friday, June 1,
            1711); v. 2: No. 81 (Saturday, June 2, 1711)-no. 169
            (Thursday, September 13, 1711); v. 3: No. 170
            (Friday, September 14, 1711)-no. 251 (Tuesday,
            December 18, 1711); v. 4: No. 252 (Wednesday,
            December 19, 1711)-no. 321 (Saturday, March 8, 1711-
            12); v. 5: No. 322 (Monday, March 10, 1711-12)-no.
            394 (Wednesday, June 2, 1712); v. 6: No. 395
            (Tuesday, June 3, 1712)-no. 473 (Tuesday, September
            2, 1712); v. 7: No. 474 (Wednesday, September 3,
            1712)-no. 555 (Saturday, December 6, 1712); v. 8: No.
            556 (Friday, June 18, 1714)-no. 635 (Monday, December
            20, 1714).
580      ‡a Reissue. Originally published daily (except Sunday),
            1711-1712, and three times a week, 1714 (publication
            suspended between no. 555 (Dec. 6, 1712) and no. 556
            (June 18, 1714)): London : Printed for Sam. Buckley
            ... and sold by A. Baldwin ..., [1711-1714];
            principal contributors: Joseph Addison, Richard
            Steele.
500      ‡a Description based on: Vol. I; title from title page.
500      ‡a Latest volume consulted: Vol. VIII.
655  7   ‡a Periodicals ‡z England ‡y 18th century. ‡2 rbgenr
700  1   ‡a Addison, Joseph, ‡d 1672-1719.
700  1   ‡a Steele, Richard, ‡c Sir, ‡d 1672-1729.
775  1   ‡s Spectator (London, England : 1711)
```

b. The rambler

```
130  0   ‡a Rambler (London, England : 1750)
245 14   ‡a The rambler / ‡c by Samuel Johnson.
260      ‡a London : ‡b Printed by P. Dodsley, R. Owen, and other
            booksellers, ‡c 1794.
300      ‡a 4 v. : ‡b ill. ; ‡c 21 cm (8vo)
362  0   ‡a Vol. I-vol. IV.
```

```
500         ‡a Individual issues have designations: v. 1: Numb. 1
               (Tuesday, March 20, 1750)-no. 53 (Tuesday, 18 Sept.,
               1750); v. 2: No. 54 (Saturday, 22 September 1750)-no.
               105 (Tuesday, 19 March 1751); v. 3: No. 106
               (Saturday, 23 March 1751)-no. 159 (Tuesday, 24 Sept.
               1751); v. 4: Number 160 (Saturday, 28 Sept., 1751)-
               no. 208 (Saturday, 15 Mar., 1752).
580         ‡a Reissue. Originally published semi-weekly from Mar.
               20, 1750, to Mar. 14, 1752. Of the 208 numbers all
               were by Johnson except no. 10, by Hester Mulso,
               afterward Mrs. Chapone; no. 30, by Catharine Talbot;
               no. 97, by Samuel Richardson; no. 44 and 100, by
               Elizabeth Carter. Parts of no. 15 and 107 are by
               unknown correspondents.
510 4       ‡a Fleeman, J.D.  Johnson, ‡c 50.3R/26
510 4       ‡a ESTC ‡c T168396
555         ‡a Cumulative index at the end of v. 4.
500         ‡a Description based on: Vol. I; title from title page.
500         ‡a Latest volume consulted: Vol. IV.
655  7      ‡a Periodicals ‡z England ‡y 18th century. ‡2 rbgenr
700 1       ‡a Carter, Elizabeth, ‡d 1717-1806.
700 1       ‡a Chapone, ‡c Mrs. ‡q (Hester), ‡d 1727-1801.
700 1       ‡a Johnson, Samuel, ‡d 1709-1784.
700 1       ‡a Richardson, Samuel, ‡d 1689-1761.
700 1       ‡a Talbot, Catherine, ‡d 1721-1770.
775 1       ‡s Rambler (London, England : 1750)
```

J5.2. Republication of two bibliographically related (earlier/later) serials, with title page

```
130 0       ‡a Gossip (London, England : 1821)
245 14      ‡a The gossip : ‡b a series of original essays and
               letters, literary, historical and critical,
               descriptive sketches, anecdotes and original poetry.
246 1       ‡i Some individual issues have caption title: ‡a Gossip
               ‡f Mar. 3-June 30, 1821
246 1       ‡i Some individual issues have caption title: ‡a
               Literary gossip ‡f July 7-Aug. 11, 1821
260         ‡a Kentish Town [London] : ‡b J. Bennett, ‡c 1821.
300         ‡a 1 v. ; ‡c 24 cm.
362 0       ‡a No. I (Saturday, March 3, 1821)-no. XXIV (Saturday,
               August 11, 1821)
500         ‡a Designation taken from individual issues.
500         ‡a Colophon of no. 1 reads: Printed by J. Bennett, Post
               Office, Kentish Town; and published by D. Rymer,
               Broad Court, Long Acre.
500         ‡a Colophons of individual issues vary slightly.
580         ‡a Reissue of The gossip and its continuation, The
               literary gossip. Originally published weekly from
               Mar. 3-Aug. 11, 1821.
500         ‡a Description based on: No. I (Saturday, March 3,
               1821); title from title page.
500         ‡a Latest issue consulted: No. XXIV (Saturday, August
               11, 1821).
```

```
650  0    ‡a English poetry ‡y 19th century ‡x History and
             criticism ‡v Periodicals.
655  7    ‡a Poems ‡z England ‡y 19th century. ‡2 rbgenr
700  1    ‡a Rymer, D., ‡e publisher.
730 02    ‡a Literary gossip.
775  1    ‡s Gossip (London, England : 1821)
775  1    ‡s Literary gossip
```

J5.3. Reissue as a new serial

Annual cumulation

```
130  0    ‡a General magazine of arts and sciences (London,
             England : Cumulation)
245 14    ‡a The general magazine of arts and sciences : ‡b
             philosophical, philological, mathematical, and
             mechanical ... / ‡c by Benjamin Martin.
246  1    ‡i Also known as: ‡a Martin's magazine
260       ‡a London : ‡b Printed for W. Owen, at Homer's Head, in
             Fleet-street, ‡c MDCCLV-MDCCLXV [1775-1765]
300       ‡a 14 v. : ‡b ill., music ; ‡c 22 cm (8vo)
310       ‡a Annual (Cumulation)
362  0    ‡a Vol. I (1755)-
362  1    ‡a Ceased in 1765. ‡z See NCBEL.
500       ‡a Editor: Benjamin Martin.
500       ‡a General title pages from v. 1, pt. 1, and from v. 14
             in red and black.
500       ‡a The cumulation is divided into six parts, each with
             individual title; parts 1-4 published in two volumes
             each; part 5 in four volumes; and, part 6 in a single
             volume. A final volume was added to the series.
             Volumes and parts are individually dated, with dates
             differing from the general title page. The dates
             range from 1755 (the general title page to Part I),
             to 1759 (the first volume of each subsequent part),
             to 1763 (the second volumes of parts 1-2) and 1764
             (the second volumes of parts 3-4). The first two
             volumes of part 5 are dated 1759, the last two, 1764.
             Part 6 and the final volume are dated 1764.
510  4    ‡a NCBEL ‡c II, 1300
510  4    ‡a Times handlist, ‡c p. 42
510  4    ‡a Crane & Kaye ‡c 266
515       ‡a Volume II misnumbered "III."
580       ‡a Cumulates contents of monthly issues with the same
             title.
580       ‡a "Miscellaneous correspondence" also issued serially
             as a separate publication in four volumes.
500       ‡a Description based on: Vol. I (1755); title from title
             page.
500       ‡a Latest volume consulted: Vol. I (1755).
650  0    ‡a Natural history ‡v Periodicals.
650  0    ‡a English poetry ‡y 18th century ‡x History and
             criticism ‡v Periodicals.
```

```
651  0    ‡a Great Britain ‡x Economic conditions ‡y 18th century
               ‡v Periodicals.
655  7    ‡a Periodicals ‡z England ‡y 18th century. ‡2 rbgenr
655  7    ‡a Poems ‡z England ‡y 18th century. ‡2 rbgenr
700  1    ‡a Martin, Benjamin, ‡d 1705-1782, ‡e ed.
730 02    ‡a Miscellaneous correspondence in prose and verse. ‡n
               [Part VI].
740 02    ‡a Young gentleman and lady's philosophy. ‡n Part I.
740 02    ‡a Natural history of England. ‡n Part II.
740 02    ‡a Philological arts and sciences. ‡n Part III.
740 02    ‡a Institutes of arithmetic, algebra, fluxions,
               geometry, and mechanics. ‡n Part IV.
740 02    ‡a Biographia philosophia. ‡n Part V.
787  1    ‡t General magazine of arts and sciences (London,
               England : Monthly)
787  1    ‡t Miscellaneous correspondence.
```

Glossary

This glossary is intended to supplement the glossary in AACR2, Appendix D. The terms included here are either lacking in AACR2, or, though present there, require some amendment to accommodate these rules to the description of printed serials in special collections.

Added title page title. A title appearing on a title page that has not been chosen as the chief source of information.

Analytical title page. The title page of an individual work in a collection or series.

Bibliographic description. A set of bibliographic data recording and identifying a serial, i.e., the description that begins with the title proper and ends with the last note.

Chief title. The distinguishing word or sequence of words that names a serial, as given on the title page (or substitute). This definition excludes alternative titles, parallel titles, other title information, and subsidiary title information preceding the chief title on the title page, such exclusion resulting usually in a short title. *See also* **Title proper**.

Chronogram. A phrase, sentence, or other text in which the numeric values of certain letters (usually distinguished typographically) express a date when added together.

Collected issues. Issues of a serial, previously published singly, which have been reissued as one or more volumes, usually with volume title page(s). The content of individual issues within the volume(s) has not been edited, expanded, or otherwise rearranged.

Cover title. A title printed on the cover of an item as issued.

Coverage date. A date reflecting the coverage of the contents of an item; distinct from the date of publication.

Device. A printed design, generally symbolic, emblematic, or pictorial rather than textual, used to identify a printer, bookseller, or publisher. To be distinguished from a logo that renders a name as a stylized, primarily textual design.

Distinctive title. A title that appears in addition to, or in place of, the title proper, is unique to a serial issue, and is often related to the topic or theme of that issue.

Edition. 1. All copies resulting from a single job of typographical composition. 2. For serials, may refer to a publication issued concurrently, or nearly so, with other versions of the same serial, sharing with those other editions the same, similar, or related contents, usually bearing the same title (or the same title in a different language), and intended for a specific audience. Examples include local or geographic editions (e.g., Eastern edition), language editions (e.g., French edition), special format editions (e.g., Braille edition), etc. Refers to an entire serial. *See also* **Reissue**.

Editor. One who prepares for publication a work not exclusively his or her own. (For special aspects of editorship in early serials, see 1E1.2n.)

Facsimile reproduction. A reproduction simulating the physical appearance of the original in addition to reproducing its contents exactly. More commonly used for editions of modern trade serials. *See also* **Reissue**.

Fluctuating title. A fluctuating title is one that changes back and forth on a regular or irregular basis. An intentional title change is not treated as a fluctuating title.

Illustration. A pictorial, diagrammatic, or other graphic representation occurring within a serial, excepting minor decorative elements such as vignettes, head- and tail-pieces, historiated initials, and printers' ornaments.

Issue. 1. A single unit published or distributed sequentially as part of a serial title. An issue may be part of a larger bibliographic unit (e.g., a single number of a weekly journal), or may comprise a complete volume (e.g., an annual report). Issues are usually published at regular intervals, and generally bear chronologic and/or numeric information. 2. A group of published copies that constitutes a consciously planned publishing unit, distinguishable from other groups of published copies by one or more differences designed expressly to identify the group as a discrete unit.

Newspaper. A serial that contains news on current events of special or general interest. The individual issues are usually numbered and appear at least once a week.

Reissue. A serial republished or reprinted at some point after the initial publication. The text is substantially unchanged, though the format, type, title, publisher, pagination, layout, prefatory matter, numbering, etc., may differ from the original. *See also* **Facsimile reproduction**.

Running title. A title or abbreviated title repeated at the head of each page or leaf. May include issue numbering.

Signature. A letter, numeral, symbol, or a group of such characters, printed at the foot of the rectos of the first few leaves of an intended gathering for the purpose of aiding binders in correctly assembling the sections.

Title proper. The chief title of a serial, together with any title information preceding the chief title and any alternative title. This definition excludes parallel titles and any other title information following the chief title. *See also* **Chief title**.

Volume title page. A page that contains the title and numbering for an entire volume, rather than for a specific issue.

LIST OF WORKS CITED

ALA-LC Romanization Tables: Transliteration Schemes for Non-Roman Scripts. 1997 ed. Washington, D.C.: Cataloging Distribution Service, Library of Congress, 1997 (and updates). Also available online at http://lcweb.loc.gov/catdir/cpso/roman.html

Anglo-American Cataloguing Rules. Joint Steering Committee for Revision of AACR. 2nd ed., 2002 revision. Ottawa: Canadian Library Association; Chicago: American Library Association, 2002 (and updates).

Art & Architecture Thesaurus Online. http://www.getty.edu/research/conducting_research/vocabularies/aat/

BIBCO Core Record Standards. Washington, D.C.: Program for Cooperative Cataloging, Library of Congress. http://www.loc.gov/catdir/pcc/bibco/coreintro.html

Bibliographic Description of Rare Books. Washington, D.C.: Office for Descriptive Cataloging Policy, Processing Services, Library of Congress, 1981.

Cappelli, Adriano. *Cronologia, Cronografia e Calendario Perpetuo*. 6. ed. Milano: Ulrico Hoepli, 1988.

Cheney, C.R. *Handbook of Dates for Students of English History*. New ed., revised by Michael Jones. Cambridge; New York: Cambridge University Press, 2004.

The Chicago Manual of Style. 15th ed. Chicago: Chicago University Press, 2003.

"Collection-Level Cataloging." *Cataloging Service Bulletin* 78 (Fall 1997): 8-28.

CONSER Cataloging Manual. Washington, D.C.: Cataloging Distribution Service, Library of Congress, 2002 (and updates).

CONSER Editing Guide. Washington, D.C.: Serial Record Division, Library of Congress, 1994 (and updates).

Describing Archives: A Content Standard. Chicago: Society of American Archivists, 2004.

Descriptive Cataloging of Rare Books. 2nd ed. Washington, D.C.: Cataloging Distribution Service, Library of Congress, 1991.

Descriptive Cataloging of Rare Materials (Books). Bibliographic Standards Committee, Rare Books and Manuscripts Section, Association of College and Research Libraries, in collaboration with the Cataloging Policy and Support Office of the Library of Congress. Washington, D.C.: Cataloging Distribution Service, Library of Congress, 2007.

Functional Requirements for Bibliographic Records. IFLA Study Group on the Functional Requirements for Bibliographic Records. München: K.G. Saur, 1998. Also available online at http://www.ifla.org/VII/s13/frbr/

ISBD(A): International Standard Bibliographic Description for Older Monographic Publications (Antiquarian). 2nd rev. ed. München: K.G. Saur, 1991. Also available online at http://www.ifla.org/VII/s13/pubs/isbda.htm

Library of Congress Rule Interpretations. 2nd ed. Washington, D.C.: Cataloging Distribution Service, Library of Congress, 1989 (and updates).

Library of Congress Subject Headings. 30th ed. Washington, D.C.: Cataloging Distribution Service, Library of Congress, 2007.

MARC 21 Format for Bibliographic Data. Network Development and MARC Standards Office, Library of Congress, in cooperation with Standards and Support, National Library of Canada. 1999 ed. Washington, D.C.: Cataloging Distribution Service, Library of Congress, 1999 (and updates). Also available online at http://www.loc.gov/marc/bibliographic/ecbdhome.html

Merriam-Webster's Collegiate Dictionary. 11th ed. Springfield, Mass.: Merriam-Webster, 2003.

"Rare Serials." *Cataloging Service Bulletin* 26 (Fall 1984): 21-25.

RBMS Controlled Vocabularies: Controlled Vocabularies for Use in Rare Book and Special Collections Cataloging. http://www.rbms.info/committees/bibliographic_standards/controlled_vocabularies/

Roe, Kathleen. *Arranging and Describing Archives and Manuscripts*. Chicago: Society of American Archivists, 2005.

Svenonius, Elaine. *The Intellectual Foundation of Information Organization*. Cambridge: The MIT Press, 2000.

Tanselle, G. Thomas. "The Bibliographical Concepts of Issue and State." *Papers of the Bibliographical Society of America* 69 (1975): 17-66.

Thesaurus for Graphic Materials. http://lcweb2.loc.gov/pp/tgmhtml/tgmabt.html

VanWingen, Peter M., and Belinda D. Urquiza. *Standard Citation Forms for Published Bibliographies and Catalogs Used in Rare Book Cataloging.* In collaboration with the Bibliographic Standards Committee, Rare Books and Manuscripts Section, Association of College and Research Libraries. 2nd ed. Washington, D.C.: Cataloging Distribution Service, Library of Congress, 1996 (and updates).

INDEX

Symbols

A

C

K

Key-title: 8C

L

LCRI: II.1, VII
Labels: 4A5
    as source of information: 6A2.4
Lacunae: 0G6.3
Lady Day dating: 4D2.4n
Language. *See also* Multilingual items
    of adaptations, notes on: 7B2
    of description: 0F
    of parallel titles: 1C2
    preferences in DCRM(S): V
Leader and directory values: Appendix B4
Letter forms: Appendix G1-G2
Letters (alphabetic). *See also* E (letter of alphabet), I (letter of alphabet); J (letter of alphabet); O (letter of alphabet), Thorn (letter of alphabet) U (letter of alphabet), V (letter of alphabet); W (letter of alphabet)
    modified. *See* Diacritical marks
    substituted by punctuation: 0G3.7
    transcription of: 0G1.1
    turned: 0G7.2
Levels of description
    collection: X.1.1, Appendix A3, Appendix B
    considerations in choosing: X.2
    full: Appendix A2
    item: X.1.1
    minimal: Appendix A4, Appendix D
    resources available to maintain: X.2.2
    serials vs. monographs: X.1.3, X.2.5
Library of Congress Rule Interpretations (LCRI). *See* LCRI
Library's holdings, notes on. *See* Copy-specific notes; Local notes
Ligatures: 0G1.1
Limitation, statement of: 7B8.2-7B8.4
Line endings: 0G3.6

Descriptive Cataloging of Rare Materials (Serials)

prescribed punctuation: 3A2

reissues: Appendix J2.3

series designation: 3F2

supplied information: 3C6, 3D

volume title page present: 3G

Numbers. *See also* Standard numbers

Numbers associated with item

notes on: 7B20

within series. *See* Series numbering

Numerals. *See* Arabic numerals; Roman numerals

O

O (letter of alphabet), superscript: Appendix G2

Obsolete place names. *See* Archaic place names

Old Style calendar. *See* Dates: Julian/Old Style

Omission, marks of: 0G3.5, 0G5.1, 0G6.3, 1B6.4. *See also* Omissions

omit without using: 0E, 0G, 0G3.4, 0G5.2-0G5.3, 1A2.2, 1E3, 7A5.2

Omissions: III.2.2, 0G5

from chief source of information: 0G4.1, 0G5.3

from edition statements: 2B7.2

from minimal-level records: Appendix D3.3

from numbering area: 3C2

from other title information: 1D3.3, 1D5

from parallel series titles: 6C2

from place of publication, distribution, etc.: 4B6.2, 4B13.2

from publisher, distributor, etc.: 4C2, 4C6.2, 4C11.2

from series information: 6C2, 6D2, 6E2.3, 6G2, 6G3.3, 6H2-6H3

from series titles: 6C2

from statements of responsibility: 1E1.2, 1E5, 1E8, 1E14.3

from title proper: 1A2.2, 1B6.4

Optional treatments in rules: IV, X. *See also* Alternative rules

abridgments: 1D5, 1E14.3

accompanying material: 5E1.2

bibliographic format: 5D1.3

bibliographic history: 7B7.1.2, 7B7.4.1

continuously paged serials: 5B3

date of publication, distribution, etc.: 4D4.3

P

Q

R

Descriptive Cataloging of Rare Materials (Serials)

S

Silent omissions. *See* Omission, marks of: omit without using

Simultaneous editions: 7B7.6

Sine loco: 4B12.4

Sine nomine: 4C9

Size: 5D

S.l. See Sine loco

s.n. See Sine nomine

Sophisticated copies. *See* Made-up copies

Sources of information: 0D. *See also* Chief source of information; Prescribed
      sources of information

    covers as prescribed: 0Dn, 6A2.1n

    dust jackets: IX.2, 0D

    interpolations to: 7A3

    title proper: 1B2

Spaces. *See* Prescribed punctuation

Spacing: 0G4

    abbreviations, initials, and initialisms: 0G10, Appendix F2 (0G10)

    omissions: 0G5

    in title proper: 0G4.2, Appendix F2 (0G4.2)

    title access points: Appendix F2 (0G10)

Special characters in edition statements: 2B3

Special collections cataloging: Appendix A8

Spelling, preferred authority for: VI

Spellings, variant. *See* Variant spellings

Split titles: 7B7.3

Square brackets: Preface, 0E, Appendix B (245). *See also* Prescribed punctuation

    adjacent elements: 0G6.4-0G6.5

    chronological designation: 3C4, 3C5

    description of imperfect copies: 0G6.3

    designation lacking in first volume or issue: 3D

    devised titles: 1B4, Appendix B4 (245)

    in notes: 7A3

    interpolations and corrections: 0G6, 0G7.1, 0G8.2, 1E9, 3H, 4 *passim*, 7A3,
        Appendix G3

    replaced by parentheses or omitted in transcription: 0G3.5

    romanized text, not used with: 0F2

    standard number and terms of availability area, not used: 8A2

    supplied words: 1E9, 2B3.2

V

V (letter of alphabet): Appendix G4.1
    transcription of: 0G2.2, Appendix G4.2
Variant forms of name: 7B6.6
Variant forms of title. *See* Titles: variant
Variant spellings: 0G4.3, 0G7.1
    rules for title access points: Appendix F2 (0G7.1)
Variant titles. *See* Titles: variant.
Variants
    variations requiring new records: Appendix E
    published references and: 7B17.2
Virgules: 0G3.5
Volume title pages: 0B2.1, 3G, Appendix F2 (7B4-7B5)
    definition of: Glossary
Volumes
    bibliographic different from physical: 5B
    used as other title information: 1D4

W

W (letter of alphabet): Appendix G4.1, Appendix G5.1
    transcription: Appendix G5.2
Width: 5D2. *See also* Dimensions
"With" notes: *See* Required notes: "With"
Words or phrases
    as names: 7B6.6
    as part of title proper: 1B1.4
    edition area: 2C2
    edition statement: 2B2
    in date of publication: 4D1.3
    in subseries: 6H2
    spacing between: 0G4.2
    spacing within: 0G4.1
    with place of publication: 4B2